# Keto Chaffles Cookbook

## Simple, Sweet and Savory Low Carb Chaffles to Boost Fat Burning and Reverse Disease

**By Stephanie Kelly**

# Table of Content

# Welcome to the Keto Chaffle World!

Hello friend!
I'm thrilled that you are here in my world of love –my newest cookbook to my writings.

I'm excited about "chaffles" –a fantastic replacement for waffles on the keto diet. Dieting the low-carb style just got more interesting, and I'm all about chaffles these days. Hence, my share with you on all that I have been up to with chaffles these past days.

Think of how much we would have missed from not enjoying these pieces of pastry that are excellent for different meal servings. I particularly enjoy them for desserts.

I'm eternally grateful to the person that exposed this formula of goodness. Ever since I came across the dish, I've been exploring new ways to create recipes that fit different meal types throughout the day. And would I say that I am obsessed yet? Yes, I am! I'm pumped about the many delicacies I can make out of them!

This cookbook is an assemblage of my creative work while exploring chaffles, and how well they fit into the keto diet. They are as tasty as can get, and believe me, you won't be able to get enough of them!

I write this book for every once-a-waffle lover that for the sake of reducing carbs, would no longer enjoy waffles. There's good news for you when you blend eggs and cheese to what will become a tastier version of traditional waffles.

I used to be a waffle addict. I recall my lunch breaks at work when my colleagues and I will walk down the street to our favorite, colorful waffle spot to grab a few with different toppings. We had them with ice cream, syrups, sauces, and always bought extras to freeze at home. Those came in handy during the weekends. Those days were hearty, having shared so many exciting stories over freshly made and crispy pieces of waffles. I missed out a lot when I decided to go keto. But not anymore, pal! There's fantastic news for us!

So, without much talking, I introduce you to my collection of eighty-four chaffle recipes that I have compiled to spark up some light in your dietary lifestyle. I share recipes that I have tried, tested, and enjoyed. Options that take you through the day from breakfast to dinner and desserts. Many offerings to last you for the entire year!

Making chaffles is one of the most comfortable things to do, and if you have older kids, they can treat you to some decadent pieces. Hence, I make sure to keep the recipes straightforward to make while giving you the flexibility to tweak the ingredients to fit your desires. However, ingredient swapping should be exact replacements. For example, you may swap cheeses by their identical kinds to give you the results that I desire for you to achieve.

Therefore, to get things kicking in already, how about you take a moment to scan through the recipes and start gathering your ingredients. I promise you that it will be a fun ride as you enjoy these crispy pieces. Do check out my tips and tricks for making the crunchiest chaffles in the following pages. They will prep you ahead for your first make.

Until I meet you at the recipe section, take a more in-depth read into how well keto and chaffles blend. I hope to be supporting your keto lifestyle for many days to come. Have fun turning out loads and loads of crunchy, delicious chaffles while making sure to share them with others.

Cheers to many days of warm, crispy chaffles and their decadent accompaniments!

# Chapter 1 Brief Dive into The Ketogenic Diet

## Grasping the Keto Diet

I enjoy learning about people's experiences and how they have achieved success from balancing fats with proteins and carbs. I learn from beginner dieters and experienced ones alike.

If you are new to the diet, are you struggling with balancing the macro proportions to help you reach success? I'll break it down for you.

You see, the Keto diet is one of the most embraced diets in recent times and one of the easiest to practice. By sticking to a standard ratio of eighty percent (80%) or more healthy fats, between twenty and thirty-five percent (20% -35%) of proteins and not more than ten percent (10%) of carbs in every meal, the body stands a better chance of reaching ketosis.

I like to keep this ratio at heart, and while I might not be precisely accurate on the percentage proportions in every meal, I make sure to be approximately right.

This practice brings me to two of my surefire ways to hit success on the keto diet.

1) I ensure to be comfortable and have fun with my diet above all things. By this practice, I aid myself to enjoy the diet instead of looking at it as a chore. This way is one takeaway that I believe you should add to your bookcase.

2) I make sure to eat healthy always. Now, up to date, I see many unhealthy practices on the internet that gear people away from the keto diet either knowingly or unknowingly. I term these practices "dirty keto." The keto diet isn't about consuming any fats but healthy ones that are sourced from natural ingredients. And in this case, since we will be deriving many fats from chaffles, it pays right to use healthy ingredients. For

success, I ensure to use organic, grass-fed, and non-GMO ingredients so that I am extracting necessary nutrients in their most natural forms.

By playing safe with these two points, I believe that you are headed for massive success soon.

# Understanding the Love Affair Between Fats, Proteins and Carbohydrates.

I have heard many keto dieters condemn carbohydrates as if they were some dreadful ingredients. Not so! Equally like fats, proteins, and other micronutrients, carbs play an essential role in our bodies. Hence, understanding how they work with other nutrients is vital instead of condemnation.

Carbohydrates are an energy-fueling unit that the brain relies on for functioning. On a regular high-carb diet, carb reserves called glycogen to serve as the primary source of energy to the brain and other organs in the body. However, these glycogen walls break down further into sucrose (sugars), which in excess may lead to high blood sugar; hence, varying related ailments caused. On the other hand, science proves that carbohydrates tend to be an inconsistent energy-fueling unit to the brain. This effect prevents the brain from functioning steadily and, therefore, the need for more carb intake to keep up with a smooth work.

After much research to curb this problem, the keto diet was formulated. While the body falls back on carbs to provide energy when in excess, fats were realized to be an alternative and more sustainable fueling unit. By feeding on more fats and fewer carbs, the body is restructured to source its energy from fat stores found in the liver known as ketones –a water-soluble molecule produced from fatty acids.

Hence, the keto diet's goal is to push the body to provide more ketones than glycogen, which implies the dietary ratio stated earlier.

Meanwhile, how do proteins play in? Although we focus on fats in this case, the body must still feed on a balanced diet with the necessary nutrients playing in. Proteins are very crucial for growth, and so, a monitored amount in every meal must be included.

Proteins break down into amino acids, which will often aid with muscle, bone, skin, nail, and cartilage building. However, an excess intake on the keto diet will quickly drive you out of ketosis as amino acids eventually increase the amount of insulin in the body.

# Understanding the Correlation Between Calories and Ketosis

Have you ever heard not to count calories on the keto diet?

I'll explain it.

Calories are the amounts of energy present in your food, which means the amounts of energy that you derive from the foods that you eat. Fats, proteins, and carbs contribute to the calorie build in the body with different levels of contribution. For instance:

1 gram of carbohydrate = 4 calories = 4 units of energy

1 gram of protein = 4 calories = 4 units of energy

1 gram of fat = 9 calories = 9 units of energy

Throughout the day, every day, the body uses energy for smooth running. Averagely, adults burn between 1800 and 2600 calories per day, which will either be sourced from the foods eaten or from your fat stores.

Now, how does this affect ketosis?

While the different macronutrients contribute to calorie build in the body, their usage style will differ. Some foods burn extra calories better than others. For example, your body will need to work extra hard to break down protein than it will for carbohydrates. On the other hand, it will be faster for fats.

On the keto diet, the goal is to increase the number of calories sourced from fats than protein and carbs to keep you in ketosis. Hence, a healthy boosting of calories through fats on the keto diet is sure to keep your ketosis.

# Blending Meals on the Keto Diet –What You Should Focus on?

By now, if you are an experienced dieter, I will agree with you that this subject comes natural to you. But, for a beginner dieter, I'll share the gem. The goal is to boost the fat stores with healthy fatty foods and reduce the intake of proteins and carbohydrates. So, here are the foods to enjoy.

- Green (above the ground) vegetables: these types of vegetables contain almost no carbs and are healthy to eat all the time. Enjoy asparagus, eggplants, tomatoes, bok choy, rapini, mushrooms, kale, green beans, cauliflower, Brussel sprouts, okra, spinach, collard greens, bell peppers, jalapeño peppers, zucchinis, olives, onions, scallions, arugula, cabbages, shallots, etc.
- Root vegetables: these a lot more carb-concentrated than green vegetables. So, I will instead have them minimally. Swap all the tubers on a regular diet with parsnips, turnips, rutabagas, celeriac, pumpkin, radishes, butternut squash.
- Healthy fats: enjoy tasty fat options from olive oil, coconut oil, avocados, grass-fed butter, heavy cream, cheeses, unsweetened almond milk, unsweetened coconut milk, unsweetened cashew milk, etc.
- Protein: As explained earlier, you may eat a moderation of proteins on the keto diet. Follow the daily proportional requirement as you consume red meats, poultry, seafood, tofu, tempeh, soy chorizo, low-carb protein powders.
- Seeds and nuts: another option to derive fats. Enjoy almonds, pistachios, cashew

nuts, peanuts, macadamia nuts, sunflower seeds, walnuts, hemp seeds, pumpkin seeds, sesame seeds, chia seeds, peanut butter, etc.

- Herbs, spices, and seasonings: many herbs and natural seasonings are welcome on the keto diet. Flavor your foods with salt, black pepper, turmeric, coriander, garlic, ginger, basil, dill, tarragon oregano, cloves, bay leaves, parsley, rosemary, marjoram, thyme, white pepper, cinnamon, pumpkin spice, chives, red curry, cumin, etc.
- Low-carb fruits: these are the only fruits allowed on the keto diet because many others are loaded with sugars. Eat avocados, blueberries, raspberries, strawberries, blackberries, goji berries, coconut, and olives.
- Safe and sugar-free condiments: for regular sugars and sauces, you may swap them with sugar-free versions of maple syrup, mustard, salsa, marinara sauce, mayonnaise, Worcestershire sauce, tamarind sauce, homemade pesto, vinegar, lemon juice, chimichurri, etc.
- Drinks: enjoy drinking water, tea, latte, coffee, berry smoothies, lassi, low-carb wines, fresh low-carb fruit juices, etc. If you must add milk to your drinks, use unsweetened nut and seed milk.

# Chapter 2 Embracing Chaffles into Our Diet

The internet is going crazy about one of the newest additions to the keto family, "CHAFFLES." Thanks to many food bloggers that have taken hold of this trend and coined out many ways to make chaffles.

Like every other addition that has come into the keto lifestyle, I find chaffles to be a pleasing idea. It doesn't only help us reach ketosis better; it is tastier than regular waffles, which makes non-keto dieters adopt this style of waffle-making too.

## What is Chaffles?

*Like waffles with a "W," chaffles is merely derived from the combination of cheese and eggs to make a waffle look alike. Hence, the name chaffles. I believe cheese replaces the "W" with "CH."*

Nothing more gets you the best pieces of chaffles than working with one or two eggs mixed with cheeses that quickly melt. So far, many attest to cheddar and mozzarella cheeses being the best options for making chaffles. I find that to work for me, too, but in the recipes below, you'll see that I incorporate other types of cheeses for some flare.

Once this basic formula is adopted well, you are free to add other keto-based ingredients to improve the texture or flavor as you desire. There are no limits to what you can make with chaffles; your best chaffle is you being unique again.

# Why Chaffles?

We all loved waffles at one point in our lives, didn't we? However, the keto diet will not accommodate the consumption of regular flour, milk, and sugars.

So, here comes in chaffles! A waffle replacement that uses the technology of making cheese omelet but would use a waffle machine to fry the combination instead. The outcome is a lighter, richer, and crispier version of a regular waffle.

Afterward, these pieces of "pastry" can be enjoyed with low-carb toppings for maximum satisfaction.

Grasping the ideology of chaffles is this simple, and I can guarantee that there is no failing with these ones.

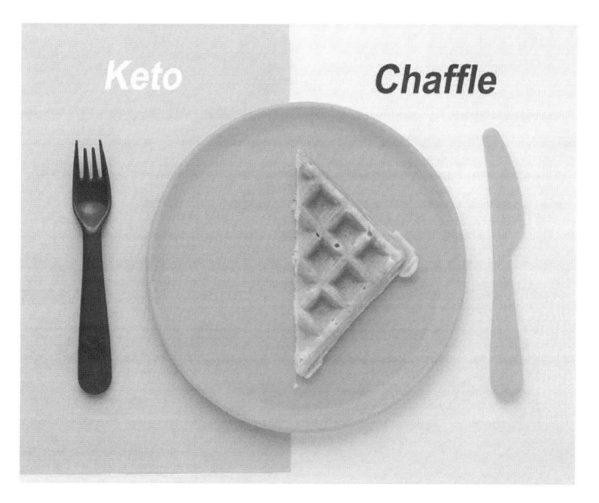

# The Magical Effect When Keto Meets Chaffles

Regularly, keto dieters lookout for ways to be accurate on the diet while searching for ways to make life easier at that.

Chaffles are one of those foods that bring on a stimulating effect to the low-carb lifestyle. I find them to be an easy fix, and thankfully, they can be enjoyed different times of the day. In the recipes below, I share many ways to make and use chaffles –for breakfast through to dinner, snacks, and desserts.

Meanwhile, while I found waffles to be addictive back then, I would say chaffles are waffles on steroids. They are moreish! Now, there isn't the need to deal with bulky, flour stuffed pastries when cheese and egg offer a better version.

This blend, therefore, makes dieting simpler as chaffles are enriched with healthy fats and mostly with no carbs. Reaching ketosis just got easier!

Finally, they are convenient for prep-ahead meals. And we know how prepping meals aids with effective keto dieting. Chaffles can be frozen for later use, and they taste excellent when warmed and enjoyed later.

Once you are hooked on chaffles, they will become a crucial part of your feeding because of the benefits that they bring. I have been making them continuously for weeks and thinking of creating a second cookbook of my new chaffle discoveries.

# How to Make Chaffles?

### Equipment and Ingredients Discussed

Making chaffles requires five simple steps and nothing more than a waffle maker for flat chaffles and a waffle bowl maker for chaffle bowls.

To make chaffles, you will need two necessary ingredients –eggs and cheese. My preferred cheeses are cheddar cheese or mozzarella cheese. These melt quickly, making them the go-to for most recipes. Meanwhile, always ensure that your cheeses are finely grated or thinly sliced for use.

Now, to make a standard chaffle:

- First, preheat your waffle maker until adequately hot.
- Meanwhile, in a bowl, mix the egg with cheese on hand until well combined.
- Open the iron, pour in a quarter or half of the mixture, and close.
- Cook the chaffle for 5 to 7 minutes or until it is crispy.
- Transfer the chaffle to a plate and allow cooling before serving.

# 12 Tips for Making the Best Chaffles

My surefire ways to turn out the crispiest of chaffles:

- **Preheat Well:** Yes! It sounds obvious to preheat the waffle iron before usage. However, preheating the iron moderately will not get your chaffles as crispy as you will like. The best way to preheat before cooking is to ensure that the iron is very hot.
- **Not-So-Cheesy:** Will you prefer to have your chaffles less cheesy? Then, use mozzarella cheese.
- **Not-So Eggy:** If you aren't comfortable with the smell of eggs in your chaffles, try using egg whites instead of egg yolks or whole eggs.

- **To Shred Or To Slice:** Many recipes call for shredded cheese when making chaffles, but I find sliced cheeses to offer crispier pieces. While I stick with mostly shredded cheese for convenience's sake, be at ease to use sliced cheese in the same quantity. When using sliced cheeses, arrange two to four pieces in the waffle iron, top with the beaten eggs, and some slices of the cheese. Cover and cook until crispy.
- **Shallower Irons:** For better crisps on your chaffles, use shallower waffle irons as they cook easier and faster.
- **Layering:** Don't fill up the waffle iron with too much batter. Work between a quarter and a half cup of total ingredients per batch for correctly done chaffles.
- **Patience:** It is a virtue even when making chaffles. For the best results, allow the chaffles to sit in the iron for 5 to 7 minutes before serving.
- **No Peeking:** 7 minutes isn't too much of a time to wait for the outcome of your chaffles, in my opinion. Opening the iron and checking on the chaffle before it is done stands you a worse chance of ruining it.
- **Crispy Cooling:** For better crisp, I find that allowing the chaffles to cool further after they are transferred to a plate aids a lot.
- **Easy Cleaning:** For the best cleanup, wet a paper towel and wipe the inner parts of the iron clean while still warm. Kindly note that the iron should be warm but not hot!
- **Brush It:** Also, use a clean toothbrush to clean between the iron's teeth for a thorough cleanup. You may also use a dry, rough sponge to clean the iron while it is still warm
- **Never Make Small Quantities:** Because you and others will want more.

Basic Flavored Chaffles

# Chapter 3 Basic Flavored Chaffles

## Simple Chaffle

Prep time: 5 minutes | Cook time: 14 minutes | Serves: 2

### Ingredients:

- ½ cup thinly sliced cheddar cheese
- 1 small egg, beaten

### Instructions:

1. Preheat the waffle iron.
2. Open the iron and lay 1/8 of the cheddar cheese in the waffle, top with half of the egg, and then another 1/8 of the cheese.
3. Close and cook until crispy, 5 to 7 minutes.
4. Remove onto a plate and cool further.
5. Make a second chaffle with the remaining ingredients in the same manner.
6. Enjoy after.

### Nutrition Facts per Serving

Calories 138 | Fats 7.19g | Carbs 7.65g | Net Carbs 7.65g | Protein 10.68g

# Zucchini-Parsley Chaffles

Prep time: 10 minutes | Cook time: 28 minutes | Serves: 4

## Ingredients:

- 2 small zucchinis, grated
- 1 large egg, beaten
- ½ cup finely grated mozzarella cheese
- 2 tbsp finely grated Parmesan cheese
- 1/8 tsp dried basil
- 1/8 tsp freshly ground black pepper to taste

## Instructions:

1. Preheat the waffle iron.
2. Meanwhile, in a medium bowl, mix all the ingredients.
3. Open the iron, pour in a quarter cup of the mixture, close the iron, and cook for 6 to 7 minutes or until crispy.
4. Remove the chaffle, plate and set aside.
5. Make the three more chaffles in the same manner, using the remaining ingredients.
6. Allow cooling and serve after.

## Nutrition Facts per Serving

Calories 58 | Fats 4.06g | Carbs 1.36g | Net Carbs 1.16g | Protein 4g

# Creamy Rich Chaffles

Prep time: 5 minutes | Cook time: 28 minutes | Serves: 4

## Ingredients:

- 1 egg, beaten
- ½ cup shredded mozzarella cheese
- 2 tbsp almond flour
- 2 tbsp cream cheese, softened
- ¾ tsp baking powder
- 3 tbsp water

## Instructions:

1. Preheat the waffle iron.
2. Meanwhile, in a medium bowl, mix all the ingredients.
3. Open the iron, pour in a quarter cup of the mixture, close the iron, and cook for 6 to 7 minutes or until crispy.
4. Remove the chaffle, plate and set aside.
5. Make three more chaffles in the same manner using the remaining ingredients.
6. Allow cooling and serve after.

## Nutrition Facts per Serving

Calories 98 | Fats 4.54g | Carbs 1.98g | Net Carbs 1.38g | Protein 12.38g

# Bacon- Jalapeño Chaffles

Prep time: 10 minutes | Cook time: 28 minutes | Serves: 4

## Ingredients:

- 1 egg, beaten
- ½ cup finely grated Gruyere cheese
- ¼ jalapeño pepper, deseeded and minced
- 2 tbsp finely chopped cooked bacon

## Instructions:

1. Preheat the waffle iron.
2. Meanwhile, in a medium bowl, mix all the ingredients.
3. Open the iron, pour in ¼ cup of the mixture, close the iron, and cook for 6 to 7 minutes or until crispy.
4. Remove the chaffle onto a plate and set aside.
5. Make three more chaffles using the remaining ingredients.
6. Allow cooling and serve after.

## Nutrition Facts per Serving

Calories 83 | Fats 5.86g | Carbs 2.37g | Net Carbs 2.17g | Protein 5.47g

# Light Parmesan Chaffles

Prep time: 10 minutes | Cook time: 28 minutes | Serves: 4

## Ingredients:

- 1 egg, beaten
- ½ tsp ground flaxseed
- ¼ tsp baking powder
- 1/3 cup finely grated cheddar cheese
- ¼ cup finely grated Parmesan cheese

## Instructions:

1. Preheat the waffle iron.
2. Meanwhile, in a medium bowl, mix all the ingredients except the Parmesan cheese.
3. Open the iron and sprinkle a little of the Parmesan cheese in the bottom. Pour on ¼ cup of the mixed ingredients and top with a little more of the Parmesan cheese.
4. Close the iron and cook until crispy, 6 to 7 minutes.
5. Remove the chaffle onto a plate and set aside.
6. Make three more chaffles using the remaining ingredients in the same manner.
7. Allow cooling and serve after.

## Nutrition Facts per Serving

Calories 119 | Fats 5.62g | Carbs 7.36g | Net Carbs 7.26g | Protein 9.72g

# Bacon Swiss Chaffles

Prep time: 5 minutes | Cook time: 28 minutes | Serves: 4

## Ingredients:

- 1 egg, beaten
- 2 tbsp finely chopped cooked bacon
- ½ cup finely grated Swiss cheese

## Instructions:

1. Preheat the waffle iron.
2. Meanwhile, in a medium bowl, mix all the ingredients.
3. Open the iron, pour in a quarter of the mixture, cover, and cook until crispy, 6 to 7 minutes.
4. Remove the chaffle onto a plate and set aside.
5. Make three more chaffles using the remaining ingredients.
6. Allow cooling and serve after.

## Nutrition Facts per Serving

Calories 82 | Fats 5.85g | Carbs 2.1g | Net Carbs 2.0g | Protein 5.41g

# Sandwich Bread Chaffles

Prep time: 10 minutes | Cook time: 28 minutes | Serves: 4

## Ingredients:

- 1 egg, beaten
- ½ cup finely grated Swiss cheese
- 4 tbsp mayonnaise
- 3 tbsp almond flour
- ¼ tsp baking powder
- 2 tsp water
- 2 tsp maple syrup

## Instructions:

1. Preheat the waffle iron.
2. Meanwhile, in a medium bowl, mix all the ingredients until smooth batter forms.
3. Open the iron, pour in a quarter of the mixture, cover, and cook until crispy, 6 to 7 minutes.
4. Remove the chaffle onto a plate and set aside.
5. Make three more chaffles using the remaining ingredients.
6. Allow cooling and use for sandwiches.

## Nutrition Facts per Serving

Calories 85 | Fats 7.31g | Carbs 0.96g | Net Carbs 0.66g | Protein 3.85g

# Savory Broccoli Chaffles

Prep time: 10 minutes | Cook time: 28 minutes | Serves: 4

## Ingredients:

- 1 cup riced broccoli
- ¼ tsp salt
- ¼ tsp freshly ground black pepper to taste
- ¼ tsp garlic powder
- ½ tsp Italian seasoning
- 1 egg, beaten
- ½ cup finely grated mozzarella cheese
- ½ cup finely grated Parmesan cheese

## Instructions:

1. Preheat the waffle iron.
2. Meanwhile, in a medium bowl, mix all the ingredients except the Parmesan cheese.
3. Open the iron and sprinkle 1/8 of the Parmesan cheese in the bottom.
4. Pour on ¼ cup of the mixed ingredients and top with 1/8 of the Parmesan cheese.
5. Close the iron and cook until crispy, 6 to 7 minutes.
6. Remove the chaffle onto a plate and set aside.
7. Make three more chaffles using the remaining ingredients in the same manner.
8. Allow cooling and serve after.

## Nutrition Facts per Serving

Calories 90 | Fats 3.79g | Carbs 6.68g | Net Carbs 5.88g | Protein 7.63g

# Apple Pie Chaffles

Prep time: 10 minutes | Cook time: 14 minutes | Serves: 2

## Ingredients:

- ½ cup finely grated mozzarella cheese
- 1 egg, beaten
- ¼ tsp apple pie spice
- 4 butter slices for serving

## Instructions:

1. Preheat the waffle iron.
2. Open the iron, pour in half of the mozzarella cheese in the iron, top with half of the egg, and sprinkle with half of the apple pie spice.
3. Close the iron and cook until crispy, 6 to 7 minutes.
4. Remove the chaffle onto a plate and set aside.
5. Make the second chaffle with the remaining ingredients.
6. Allow cooling and serve after.

## Nutrition Facts per Serving

Calories 146 | Fats 14.73g | Carbs 0.9g | Net Carbs 0.7g | Protein 3.07g

# Cinnamon-Mozzarella Chaffles

Prep time: 10 minutes | Cook time: 14 minutes | Serves: 2

## Ingredients:

- 1 egg, beaten
- ½ cup finely grated mozzarella cheese
- ½ tsp baking powder
- 1 tbsp vanilla extract
- 1 tbsp almond flour
- ½ tsp cinnamon powder

## Instructions:

1. Preheat the waffle iron.
2. Meanwhile, in a medium bowl, mix all the ingredients until smooth batter forms.
3. Open the iron, pour in half of the mixture, cover, and cook until crispy, 6 to 7 minutes.
4. Remove the chaffle onto a plate and set aside.
5. Make the second chaffle with the remaining ingredients.
6. Allow cooling and enjoy.

## Nutrition Facts per Serving

Calories 56 | Fats 3.36g | Carbs 1.85g | Net Carbs 1.45g | Protein 3.02g

# Peanut Butter Chaffles

Prep time: 10 minutes | Cook time: 28 minutes | Serves: 4

## Ingredients:

- 2 tbsp sugar-free peanut butter powder
- 2 tbsp maple (sugar-free) syrup
- 1 egg, beaten
- ½ cup finely grated mozzarella cheese
- ¼ tsp baking powder
- ¼ tsp peanut butter extract
- 1 tbsp softened cream cheese

## Instructions:

1. Preheat the waffle iron.
2. Meanwhile, in a medium bowl, mix all the ingredients until smooth.
3. Open the iron and pour in a quarter of the mixture.
4. Close the iron and cook until crispy, 6 to 7 minutes.
5. Remove the chaffle onto a plate and set aside.
6. Make three more chaffles with the remaining batter.
7. Allow cooling and serve after.

## Nutrition Facts per Serving

Calories 102 | Fats 5.31g | Carbs 10.41g | Net Carbs 9.91g | Protein 4.08g

# Lemon-Coconut Chaffles

Prep time: 10 minutes | Cook time: 14 minutes | Serves: 2

## Ingredients:

- 2 oz cream cheese, softened
- 1 egg, beaten
- 2 tbsp coconut flour
- 2 tsp butter, melted
- 1 tsp maple (sugar-free) syrup
- 1 tsp baking powder
- ½ tsp lemon extract

## Instructions:

1. Preheat the waffle iron.
2. Meanwhile, in a medium bowl, mix all the ingredients until smooth.
3. Open the iron and pour in half of the mixture.
4. Close the iron and cook until crispy, 6 to 7 minutes.
5. Remove the chaffle onto a plate and set aside.
6. Make the second chaffle with the remaining batter.
7. Allow cooling and serve after.

## Nutrition Facts per Serving

Calories 340 | Fats 31.22g | Carbs 8.25g | Net Carbs 4.15g | Protein 9.08g

# Strawberry Chaffles

Prep time: 10 minutes | Cook time: 14 minutes | Serves: 2

## Ingredients:

- 1 egg, beaten
- 2 tbsp almond flour
- 1 (0.6 oz) pack sugar-free strawberry jello mix
- 4 oz cream cheese
- 1 tsp vanilla extract

## Instructions:

1. Preheat the waffle iron .
2. Meanwhile, in a medium bowl, whisk all the ingredients until smooth batter forms.
3. Open the iron, pour in half of the mixture, cover, and cook until crispy, 6 to 7 minutes.
4. Remove the chaffle onto a plate and set aside.
5. Make the second chaffle with the remaining batter.
6. Allow cooling and enjoy.

## Nutrition Facts per Serving

Calories 244 | Fats 21g | Carbs 2.86g | Net Carbs 2.66g | Protein 9.84g

Breakfast & Brunch

# Chapter 4 Breakfast & Brunch

## Raspberry-Yogurt Chaffle Bowl

Prep time: 10 minutes | Cook time: 14 minutes | Serves: 2

**Ingredients:**

- 1 egg, beaten
- 1 tbsp almond flour
- ¼ cup finely grated mozzarella cheese
- ¼ tsp baking powder
- 1 cup Greek yogurt
- 1 cup fresh raspberries
- 2 tbsp almonds, chopped

**Instructions:**

1. Preheat a waffle bowl maker and grease lightly with cooking spray.
2. Meanwhile, in a medium bowl, whisk all the ingredients except the yogurt, raspberries until smooth batter forms.
3. Open the iron, pour in half of the mixture, cover, and cook until crispy, 6 to 7 minutes.
4. Remove the chaffle bowl onto a plate and set aside.
5. Make the second chaffle bowl with the remaining batter.
6. To serve, divide the yogurt into the chaffle bowls and top with the raspberries and almonds.

**Nutrition Facts per Serving**

Calories 75 | Fats 3.69g | Carbs 6.95g | Net Carbs 4.85g | Protein 4.07g

# Bacon-Cheddar Biscuit Chaffle

Prep time: 10 minutes | Cook time: 28 minutes | Serves: 4

## Ingredients:

- 1 egg, beaten
- 2 tbsp almond flour
- 2 tbsp ground flaxseed
- 3 bacon slices, cooked and chopped
- ¼ cup heavy cream
- 1 ½ tbsp melted butter
- ½ cup finely grated Gruyere cheese
- ½ cup finely grated cheddar cheese
- ¼ tsp erythritol
- ½ tsp onion powder
- ½ tsp garlic salt
- ½ tbsp dried parsley
- ½ tbsp baking powder
- ¼ tsp baking soda

## Instructions:

1. Preheat the waffle iron.
2. Meanwhile, in a medium bowl, whisk all the ingredients until smooth batter forms.
3. Open the iron, pour a quarter of the mixture into the iron, close and cook until crispy, 6 to 7 minutes.
4. Remove the chaffle onto a plate and set aside.
5. Make three more Chaffles with the remaining batter.
6. Allow cooling and serve afterward.

## Nutrition Facts per Serving

Calories 397 | Fats 30.08g | Carbs 14.1g | Net Carbs 11.1g | Protein 19.09g

# Turnip Hash Brown Chaffles

Prep time: 10 minutes | Cook time: 42 minutes | Serves: 6

## Ingredients:

- 1 large turnip, peeled and shredded
- ½ medium white onion, minced
- 2 garlic cloves, pressed
- 1 cup finely grated Gouda cheese
- 2 eggs, beaten
- Salt and freshly ground black pepper to taste

## Instructions:

1. Pour the turnips in a medium safe microwave bowl, sprinkle with 1 tbsp of water, and steam in the microwave until softened, 1 to 2 minutes.
2. Remove the bowl and mix in the remaining ingredients except for a quarter cup of the Gouda cheese.
3. Preheat the waffle iron.
4. Once heated, open and sprinkle some of the reserved cheese in the iron and top with 3 tablespoons of the mixture. Close the waffle iron and cook until crispy, 5 minutes.
5. Open the lid, flip the chaffle and cook further for 2 more minutes.
6. Remove the chaffle onto a plate and set aside.
7. Make five more chaffles with the remaining batter in the same proportion.
8. Allow cooling and serve afterward.

## Nutrition Facts per Serving

Calories 230 | Fats 15.85g | Carbs 5.01g | Net Carbs 3.51g | Protein 16.57g

# BLT Chaffle Sandwiches

Prep time: 10 minutes | Cook time: 28 minutes | Serves: 2

## Ingredients:

- 1 egg, beaten
- ½ cup finely grated mozzarella cheese
- 2 scallions, finely chopped
- ½ tsp Italian seasoning
- 2 bacon slices, cooked
- 2 lettuce leaves
- 2 tomato slices
- 1 tbsp mayonnaise

## Instructions:

1. Preheat the waffle iron.
2. Meanwhile, in a medium bowl, mix the egg, mozzarella cheese, scallions, and Italian seasoning.
3. Open the iron, pour a quarter of the mixture into the iron, close and cook until crispy, 6 to 7 minutes.
4. Remove the chaffle onto a plate and set aside.
5. Make three more chaffles with the remaining batter.
6. To assemble the sandwich: on one chaffle, layer one bacon slice, one lettuce leaf, one tomato slice and top with half of the mayonnaise. Cover with another chaffle.
7. Make a second sandwich in the same manner and enjoy after.

## Nutrition Facts per Serving

Calories 114 | Fats 9.53g | Carbs 2.17g | Net Carbs 1.57g | Protein 5.06g

# Everything Bagel Chaffles

Prep time: 10 minutes | Cook time: 28 minutes | Serves: 4

## Ingredients:

- 1 egg, beaten
- ½ cup finely grated Parmesan cheese
- 1 tsp Everything Bagel seasoning

## Instructions:

1. Preheat the waffle iron.
2. In a medium bowl, mix all the ingredients.
3. Open the iron, pour in a quarter of the mixture, close, and cook until crispy, 6 to 7 minutes.
4. Remove the chaffle onto a plate and set aside.
5. Make three more chaffles, allow cooling, and enjoy after.

## Nutrition Facts per Serving

Calories 53 | Fats 1.55g | Carbs 4.08g | Net Carbs 4.08g | Protein 5.38g

# Blueberry Shortcake Chaffles

Prep time: 10 minutes | Cook time: 14 minutes | Serves: 2

## Ingredients:

- 1 egg, beaten
- 1 tbsp cream cheese, softened
- ¼ cup finely grated mozzarella cheese
- 1/4 tsp baking powder
- 4 fresh blueberries
- 1 tsp blueberry extract

## Instructions:

1. Preheat the waffle iron.
2. In a medium bowl, mix all the ingredients.
3. Open the iron, pour in half of the batter, close, and cook until crispy, 6 to 7 minutes.
4. Remove the chaffle onto a plate and set aside.
5. Make the other chaffle with the remaining batter.
6. Allow cooling and enjoy after.

## Nutrition Facts per Serving

Calories 46 | Fats 3.21g | Carbs 1.16g | Net Carbs 1.14g | Protein 2.45g

# Raspberry-Pecan Chaffles

Prep time: 10 minutes | Cook time: 14 minutes | Serves: 2

## Ingredients:

- 1 egg, beaten
- ½ cup finely grated mozzarella cheese
- 1 tbsp cream cheese, softened
- 1 tbsp sugar-free maple syrup
- ¼ tsp raspberry extract
- ¼ tsp vanilla extract
- 2 tbsp sugar-free caramel sauce for topping
- 3 tbsp chopped pecans for topping

## Instructions:

1. Preheat the waffle iron.
2. In a medium bowl, mix all the ingredients.
3. Open the iron, pour in half of the batter, close, and cook until crispy, 6 to 7 minutes.
4. Remove the chaffle onto a plate and set aside.
5. Make another chaffle with the remaining batter.
6. To serve: drizzle the caramel sauce on the chaffles and top with the pecans.

## Nutrition Facts per Serving

Calories 186 | Fats 16.3g | Carbs 3.53g | Net Carbs 2.23g | Protein 7.43g

# Pumpkin Spice Chaffles

Prep time: 10 minutes | Cook time: 14 minutes | Serves: 2

## Ingredients:

- 1 egg, beaten
- ½ tsp pumpkin pie spice
- ½ cup finely grated mozzarella cheese
- 1 tbsp sugar-free pumpkin puree

## Instructions:

1. Preheat the waffle iron.
2. In a medium bowl, mix all the ingredients.
3. Open the iron, pour in half of the batter, close, and cook until crispy, 6 to 7 minutes.
4. Remove the chaffle onto a plate and set aside.
5. Make another chaffle with the remaining batter.
6. Allow cooling and serve afterward.

## Nutrition Facts per Serving

Calories 90 | Fats 6.46g | Carbs 1.98g | Net Carbs 1.58g | Protein 5.94g

# Breakfast Spinach Ricotta Chaffles

Prep time: 10 minutes | Cook time: 28 minutes | Serves: 4

## Ingredients:

- 4 oz frozen spinach, thawed, squeezed dry
- 1 cup ricotta cheese
- 2 eggs, beaten
- ½ tsp garlic powder
- ¼ cup finely grated Pecorino Romano cheese
- ½ cup finely grated mozzarella cheese
- Salt and freshly ground black pepper to taste

## Instructions:

1. Preheat the waffle iron.
2. In a medium bowl, mix all the ingredients.
3. Open the iron, lightly grease with cooking spray and spoon in a quarter of the mixture.
4. Close the iron and cook until brown and crispy, 7 minutes.
5. Remove the chaffle onto a plate and set aside.
6. Make three more chaffles with the remaining mixture.
7. Allow cooling and serve afterward.

## Nutrition Facts per Serving

Calories 188 | Fats 13.15g | Carbs 5.06g | Net Carbs 4.06g | Protein 12.79g

# Scrambled Egg Stuffed Chaffles

Prep time: 15 minutes | Cook time: 28 minutes | Serves: 4

## Ingredients:

### For the chaffles:

- 1 cup finely grated cheddar cheese
- 2 eggs, beaten

### For the egg stuffing:

- 1 tbsp olive oil
- 4 large eggs

- 1 small green bell pepper, deseeded and chopped
- 1 small red bell pepper, deseeded and chopped
- Salt and freshly ground black pepper to taste
- 2 tbsp grated Parmesan cheese

## Instructions:

### For the chaffles:

1. Preheat the waffle iron.
2. In a medium bowl, mix the cheddar cheese and egg.
3. Open the iron, pour in a quarter of the mixture, close, and cook until crispy, 6 to 7 minutes.
4. Plate and make three more chaffles using the remaining mixture.

### For the egg stuffing:

5. Meanwhile, heat the olive oil in a medium skillet over medium heat on a stovetop.
6. In a medium bowl, beat the eggs with the bell peppers, salt, black pepper, and Parmesan cheese.
7. Pour the mixture into the skillet and scramble until set to your likeness, 2 minutes.
8. Between two chaffles, spoon half of the scrambled eggs and repeat with the second set of chaffles.
9. Serve afterward.

## Nutrition Facts per Serving:

Calories 387 | Fats 22.52g | Carbs 18.12g | Net Carbs 17.52g | Protein 27.76g

# Mixed Berry-Vanilla Chaffles

Prep time: 10 minutes | Cook time: 28 minutes | Serves: 4

## Ingredients:

- 1 egg, beaten
- ½ cup finely grated mozzarella cheese
- 1 tbsp cream cheese, softened
- 1 tbsp sugar-free maple syrup
- 2 strawberries, sliced
- 2 raspberries, slices
- ¼ tsp blackberry extract
- ¼ tsp vanilla extract
- ½ cup plain yogurt for serving

## Instructions:

1. Preheat the waffle iron.
2. In a medium bowl, mix all the ingredients except the yogurt.
3. Open the iron, lightly grease with cooking spray and pour in a quarter of the mixture.
4. Close the iron and cook until golden brown and crispy, 7 minutes.
5. Remove the chaffle onto a plate and set aside.
6. Make three more chaffles with the remaining mixture.
7. To serve: top with the yogurt and enjoy.

## Nutrition Facts per Serving:

Calories 78 | Fats 5.29g | Carbs 3.02g | Net Carbs 2.72g | Protein 4.32g

# Ham and Cheddar Chaffles

Prep time: 15 minutes | Cook time: 28 minutes | Serves: 4

## Ingredients:

- 1 cup finely shredded parsnips, steamed
- 8 oz ham, diced
- 2 eggs, beaten
- 1 ½ cups finely grated cheddar cheese
- ½ tsp garlic powder
- 2 tbsp chopped fresh parsley leaves
- ¼ tsp smoked paprika
- ½ tsp dried thyme
- Salt and freshly ground black pepper to taste

## Instructions:

1. Preheat the waffle iron.
2. In a medium bowl, mix all the ingredients.
3. Open the iron, lightly grease with cooking spray and pour in a quarter of the mixture.
4. Close the iron and cook until crispy, 7 minutes.
5. Remove the chaffle onto a plate and set aside.
6. Make three more chaffles using the remaining mixture.
7. Serve afterward.

## Nutrition Facts per Serving:

Calories 506 | Fats 24.05g | Carbs 30.02g | Net Carbs 28.22g | Protein 42.74g

# Savory Gruyere and Chives Chaffles

Prep time: 15 minutes | Cook time: 14 minutes | Serves: 2

## Ingredients:

- 2 eggs, beaten
- 1 cup finely grated Gruyere cheese
- 2 tbsp finely grated cheddar cheese
- 1/8 tsp freshly ground black pepper
- 3 tbsp minced fresh chives + more for garnishing
- 2 sunshine fried eggs for topping

## Instructions:

1. Preheat the waffle iron.
2. In a medium bowl, mix the eggs, cheeses, black pepper, and chives.
3. Open the iron and pour in half of the mixture.
4. Close the iron and cook until brown and crispy, 7 minutes.
5. Remove the chaffle onto a plate and set aside.
6. Make another chaffle using the remaining mixture.
7. Top each chaffle with one fried egg each, garnish with the chives and serve.

## Nutrition Facts per Serving:

Calories 712 | Fats 41.32g | Carbs 3.88g | Net Carbs 3.78g | Protein 23.75g

# Chicken Quesadilla Chaffle

Prep time: 10 minutes | Cook time: 14 minutes | Serves: 2

## Ingredients:

- 1 egg, beaten
- ¼ tsp taco seasoning
- 1/3 cup finely grated cheddar cheese
- 1/3 cup cooked chopped chicken

## Instructions:

1. Preheat the waffle iron.
2. In a medium bowl, mix the eggs, taco seasoning, and cheddar cheese. Add the chicken and combine well.
3. Open the iron, lightly grease with cooking spray and pour in half of the mixture.
4. Close the iron and cook until brown and crispy, 7 minutes.
5. Remove the chaffle onto a plate and set aside.
6. Make another chaffle using the remaining mixture.
7. Serve afterward.

## Nutrition Facts per Serving:

Calories 314 | Fats 20.64g | Carbs 5.71g | Net Carbs 5.71g | Protein 16.74g

# Hot Chocolate Breakfast Chaffle

Prep time: 10 minutes | Cook time: 14 minutes | Serves: 2

## Ingredients:

- 1 egg, beaten
- 2 tbsp almond flour
- 1 tbsp unsweetened cocoa powder
- 2 tbsp cream cheese, softened
- ¼ cup finely grated Monterey Jack cheese
- 2 tbsp sugar-free maple syrup
- 1 tsp vanilla extract

## Instructions:

1. Preheat the waffle iron.
2. In a medium bowl, mix all the ingredients.
3. Open the iron, lightly grease with cooking spray and pour in half of the mixture.
4. Close the iron and cook until crispy, 7 minutes.
5. Remove the chaffle onto a plate and set aside.
6. Pour the remaining batter in the iron and make the second chaffle.
7. Allow cooling and serve afterward.

## Nutrition Facts per Serving:

Calories 47 | Fats 3.67g | Carbs 1.39g | Net Carbs 0.89g | Protein 2.29g

# Chapter 5 Snacks

## Protein Vanilla Chaffle Sticks

Prep time: 10 minutes | Cook time: 28 minutes | Serves: 4

**Ingredients:**

- ½ scoop zero-carb protein powder
- 1 cup finely grated mozzarella cheese
- 2 eggs, beaten
- 1 tbsp erythritol
- ½ tsp vanilla extract

**Instructions:**

1. Preheat the waffle iron.
2. In a medium bowl, mix the protein powder, mozzarella cheese, eggs, erythritol, and vanilla extract until well combined.
3. Open the iron and pour in a quarter of the batter. Close the iron and cook until golden brown and crispy, 7 minutes.
4. Remove the chaffle onto a plate and set aside.
5. Make three more chaffles after and transfer to a plate to cool.
6. Before enjoying, slice each chaffle into 4 sticks and serve.

**Nutrition Facts per Serving:**

Calories 83 | Fats 4.56g | Carbs 2.59g | Net Carbs 2.09g | Protein 7.45g

# Keto Oreo Chaffles

Prep time: 13 minutes | Cook time: 28 minutes | Serves: 4

## Ingredients:

### For the Oreo chaffles:

- 2 eggs, beaten
- 1 cup finely grated mozzarella cheese
- 2 tbsp almond flour
- 1 tbsp unsweetened dark cocoa powder
- 2 tbsp erythritol
- 1 tbsp cream cheese, softened
- ½ tsp vanilla extract

### For the glaze:

- 1 tbsp swerve confectioner's sugar
- 1 tsp water

## Instructions:

1. Preheat the waffle iron.
2. In a medium bowl, combine all the ingredients for the Oreo chaffles until adequately mixed.
3. Open the iron and pour in a quarter of the batter. Close the iron and cook until crispy, 7 minutes.
4. Remove the chaffle onto a plate and set aside.
5. Make 3 more chaffles with the remaining batter and transfer to a plate to cool.

### For the glaze:

6. In a small bowl, whisk the swerve confectioner's sugar and water until smooth.
7. Drizzle a little of the glaze over each chaffle and serve after.

## Nutrition Facts per Serving:

Calories 50 | Fats 3.64g | Carbs 1.27g | Net Carbs 0.77g | Protein 3.4g

# Fried Pickle Chaffle Sticks

Prep time: 10 minutes | Cook time: 28 minutes | Serves: 4

## Ingredients:

- 1 egg, beaten
- ¼ cup pork rinds
- ½ cup finely grated mozzarella cheese
- ½ tbsp pickle juice
- 8 thin pickle slices, patted with a paper towel

## Instructions:

1. Preheat the waffle iron.
2. In a medium bowl, combine the egg, pork rinds, mozzarella cheese, and pickle juice.
3. Open the iron and pour in 2 tbsp of the mixture, lay two pickle slices on top, and cover with 2 tbsp of the batter.
4. Close the iron and cook until brown and crispy, 7 minutes.
5. Remove the chaffle onto a plate and set aside.
6. Make 3 more chaffles in the same manner, using the remaining ingredients.
7. Cut the chaffles into sticks and serve after with cheese dip.

## Nutrition Facts per Serving

Calories 68 | Fats 4.17g | Carbs 2.2g | Net Carbs 2.0g | Protein 5.25g

# Keto Chaffle Churro Sticks

Prep time: 10 minutes | Cook time: 28 minutes | Serves: 4

## Ingredients:

- 1 egg, beaten
- ½ cup finely grated mozzarella cheese
- 2 tbsp swerve brown sugar
- ½ tsp cinnamon powder

## Instructions:

1. Preheat the waffle iron.
2. Combine all the ingredients in a medium bowl until smooth.
3. Open the iron and pour in a quarter of the mixture. Close the iron and cook until golden brown and crispy, 7 minutes.
4. Remove the chaffle onto a plate and set aside.
5. Make 3 more chaffles with the remaining ingredients
6. Cut the chaffles into 4 sticks and serve after.

## Nutrition Facts per Serving:

Calories 45 | Fats 3.2g | Carbs 1.08g | Net Carbs 0.78g | Protein 2.95g

# Chocolate Chip Cookie Sticks

Prep time: 10 minutes | Cook time: 28 minutes | Serves: 4

## Ingredients:

- 1 tbsp melted butter
- 1/8 tsp vanilla extract
- 1 tbsp sugar-free maple syrup
- 1 egg yolk
- 1/8 tsp baking powder
- 3 tbsp almond flour
- 1 tbsp unsweetened chocolate chips

## Instructions:

1. Preheat the waffle iron.
2. Add all the ingredients to a medium bowl and mix well.
3. Open the iron and pour in a quarter of the mixture. Close the iron and cook until crispy, 7 minutes.
4. Remove the chaffle onto a plate and set aside.
5. Make 3 more chaffles with the remaining batter.
6. Cut the chaffles into sticks and serve.

## Nutrition Facts per Serving:

Calories 72 | Fats 4.46g | Carbs 0.36g | Net Carbs 0.26g | Protein 0.89g

# Sausage Ball Chaffles

Prep time: 15 minutes | Cook time: 28 minutes | Serves: 4

## Ingredients:

- 1 lb Italian sausage, crumbled
- 3 tbsp almond flour
- 2 tsp baking powder
- 1 egg, beaten
- ¼ cup finely grated Parmesan cheese
- 1 cup finely grated cheddar cheese

## Instructions:

1. Preheat the waffle iron.
2. Pour all the ingredients into a medium mixing bowl and mix well with your hands.
3. Open the iron, lightly grease with cooking spray and add 3 tbsp of the sausage mixture. Close the iron and cook for 4 minutes.
4. Open the iron, flip the chaffles and cook further for 3 minutes.
5. Remove the chaffle onto a plate and make 3 more using the rest of the mixture.
6. Cut each chaffle into sticks or quarters and enjoy after.

## Nutrition Facts per Serving:

Calories 465 | Fats 33.5g | Carbs 10.87g | Net Carbs 7.57g | Protein 32.52g

# Garlic Bread Chaffles

Prep time: 10 minutes | Cook time: 14 minutes | Serves: 2

## Ingredients:

- 1 egg, beaten
- ½ cup finely grated mozzarella cheese
- 1 tsp Italian seasoning
- ½ tsp garlic powder
- 1 tsp chive-flavored cream cheese

## Instructions:

1. Preheat the waffle iron.
2. Mix all the ingredients in a medium bowl until well combined.
3. Open the iron and add half of the mixture. Close and cook until golden brown and crispy, 7 minutes.
4. Remove the chaffle onto a plate and make a second one with the remaining batter.
5. Cut each chaffle into sticks or quarters and enjoy after.

## Nutrition Facts per Serving:

Calories 51 | Fats 3.56g | Carbs 1.57g | Net Carbs 1.27g | Protein 3.13g

# Pumpkin-Cinnamon Churro Sticks

Prep time: 10 minutes | Cook time: 14 minutes | Serves: 2

## Ingredients:

- 3 tbsp coconut flour
- ¼ cup pumpkin puree
- 1 egg, beaten
- ½ cup finely grated mozzarella cheese
- 2 tbsp sugar-free maple syrup + more for serving
- 1 tsp baking powder
- 1 tsp vanilla extract
- ½ tsp pumpkin spice seasoning
- 1/8 tsp salt
- 1 tbsp cinnamon powder

## Instructions:

1. Preheat the waffle iron.
2. Mix all the ingredients in a medium bowl until well combined.
3. Open the iron and add half of the mixture. Close and cook until golden brown and crispy, 7 minutes.
4. Remove the chaffle onto a plate and make 1 more with the remaining batter.
5. Cut each chaffle into sticks, drizzle the top with more maple syrup and serve after.

## Nutrition Facts per Serving:

Calories 219 | Fats 9.72g | Carbs 8.64g | Net Carbs 4.34g | Protein 25.27g

# Keto Chocolate Fudge Chaffle

Prep time: 10 minutes | Cook time: 14 minutes | Serves: 2

## Ingredients:

- 1 egg, beaten
- ¼ cup finely grated Gruyere cheese
- 2 tbsp unsweetened cocoa powder
- ¼ tsp baking powder
- ¼ tsp vanilla extract
- 2 tbsp erythritol
- 1 tsp almond flour
- 1 tsp heavy whipping cream
- A pinch of salt

## Instructions:

1. Preheat the waffle iron.
2. Add all the ingredients to a medium bowl and mix well.
3. Open the iron and add half of the mixture. Close and cook until golden brown and crispy, 7 minutes.
4. Remove the chaffle onto a plate and make another with the remaining batter.
5. Cut each chaffle into wedges and serve after.

## Nutrition Facts per Serving:

Calories 173 | Fats 13.08g | Carbs 3.98g | Net Carbs 2.28g | Protein 12.27g

# Guacamole Chaffle Bites

Prep time: 10 minutes | Cook time: 14 minutes | Serves: 2

## Ingredients:

- 1 large turnip, cooked and mashed
- 2 bacon slices, cooked and finely chopped
- ½ cup finely grated Monterey Jack cheese
- 1 egg, beaten
- 1 cup guacamole for topping

## Instructions:

1. Preheat the waffle iron.
2. Mix all the ingredients except for the guacamole in a medium bowl.
3. Open the iron and add half of the mixture. Close and cook for 4 minutes. Open the lid, flip the chaffle and cook further until golden brown and crispy, 3 minutes.
4. Remove the chaffle onto a plate and make another in the same manner.
5. Cut each chaffle into wedges, top with the guacamole and serve afterward.

## Nutrition Facts per Serving:

Calories 311 | Fats 22.52g | Carbs 8.29g | Net Carbs 5.79g | Protein 13.62g

# Zucchini Parmesan Chaffles

Prep time: 10 minutes | Cook time: 14 minutes | Serves: 2

## Ingredients:

- 1 cup shredded zucchini
- 1 egg, beaten
- ½ cup finely grated Parmesan cheese
- Salt and freshly ground black pepper to taste

## Instructions:

1. Preheat the waffle iron.
2. Put all the ingredients in a medium bowl and mix well.
3. Open the iron and add half of the mixture. Close and cook until crispy, 7 minutes.
4. Remove the chaffle onto a plate and make another with the remaining mixture.
5. Cut each chaffle into wedges and serve afterward.

## Nutrition Facts per Serving:

Calories 138 | Fats 9.07g | Carbs 3.81g | Net Carbs 3.71g | Protein 10.02g

# Blue Cheese Chaffle Bites

Prep time: 10 minutes | Cook time: 14 minutes | Serves: 2

## Ingredients:

- 1 egg, beaten
- ½ cup finely grated Parmesan cheese
- ¼ cup crumbled blue cheese
- 1 tsp erythritol

## Instructions:

1. Preheat the waffle iron.
2. Mix all the ingredients in a bowl.
3. Open the iron and add half of the mixture. Close and cook until crispy, 7 minutes.
4. Remove the chaffle onto a plate and make another with the remaining mixture.
5. Cut each chaffle into wedges and serve afterward.

## Nutrition Facts per Serving:

Calories 196 | Fats 13.91g | Carbs 4.03g | Net Carbs 4.03g | Protein 13.48g

# Chaffle Fruit Snacks

Prep time: 10 minutes | Cook time: 14 minutes | Serves: 2

## Ingredients:

- 1 egg, beaten
- ½ cup finely grated cheddar cheese
- ½ cup Greek yogurt for topping
- 8 raspberries and blackberries for topping

## Instructions:

1. Preheat the waffle iron.
2. Mix the egg and cheddar cheese in a medium bowl.
3. Open the iron and add half of the mixture. Close and cook until crispy, 7 minutes.
4. Remove the chaffle onto a plate and make another with the remaining mixture.
5. Cut each chaffle into wedges and arrange on a plate.
6. Top each waffle with a tablespoon of yogurt and then two berries.
7. Serve afterward.

## Nutrition Facts per Serving

Calories 207 | Fats 15.29g | Carbs 4.36g | Net Carbs 3.86g | Protein 12.91g

# Keto Belgian Sugar Chaffles

Prep time: 10 minutes | Cook time: 24 minutes | Serves: 4

## Ingredients:

- 1 egg, beaten
- 2 tbsp swerve brown sugar
- ½ tbsp butter, melted
- 1 tsp vanilla extract
- 1 cup finely grated Parmesan cheese

## Instructions:

1. Preheat the waffle iron.
2. Mix all the ingredients in a medium bowl.
3. Open the iron and pour in a quarter of the mixture. Close and cook until crispy, 6 minutes.
4. Remove the chaffle onto a plate and make 3 more with the remaining ingredients.
5. Cut each chaffle into wedges, plate, allow cooling and serve.

## Nutrition Facts per Serving

Calories 136 | Fats 9.45g | Carbs 3.69g | Net Carbs 3.69g | Protein 8.5g

# Lemon and Paprika Chaffles

Prep time: 10 minutes | Cook time: 28 minutes | Serves: 4

## Ingredients:

- 1 egg, beaten
- 1 oz cream cheese, softened
- 1/3 cup finely grated mozzarella cheese
- 1 tbsp almond flour
- 1 tsp butter, melted
- 1 tsp maple (sugar-free) syrup
- ½ tsp sweet paprika
- ½ tsp lemon extract

## Instructions:

1. Preheat the waffle iron.
2. Mix all the ingredients in a medium bowl
3. Open the iron and pour in a quarter of the mixture. Close and cook until crispy, 7 minutes.
4. Remove the chaffle onto a plate and make 3 more with the remaining mixture.
5. Cut each chaffle into wedges, plate, allow cooling and serve.

## Nutrition Facts per Serving

Calories 48 | Fats 4.22g | Carbs 0.6g | Net Carbs 0.5g | Protein 2g

# Herby Chaffle Snacks

Prep time: 10 minutes | Cook time: 28 minutes | Serves: 4

## Ingredients:

- 1 egg, beaten
- ½ cup finely grated Monterey Jack cheese
- ¼ cup finely grated Parmesan cheese
- ½ tsp dried mixed herbs

## Instructions:

1. Preheat the waffle iron.
2. Mix all the ingredients in a medium bowl
3. Open the iron and pour in a quarter of the mixture. Close and cook until crispy, 7 minutes.
4. Remove the chaffle onto a plate and make 3 more with the rest of the ingredients.
5. Cut each chaffle into wedges and plate.
6. Allow cooling and serve.

## Nutrition Facts per Serving

Calories 96 | Fats 6.29g | Carbs 2.19g | Net Carbs 2.19g | Protein 7.42g

Lunch & Dinner

# Chapter 6 Lunch & Dinner

## Pizza Chaffles

Prep time: 10 minutes | Cook time: 28 minutes | Serves: 4

**Ingredients:**

- 1 egg, beaten
- ½ cup finely grated mozzarella cheese + extra for topping
- 1 tbsp pizza sauce
- 1 tbsp almond flour
- 4 pepperoni slices

**Instructions:**

1. Preheat the waffle iron.
2. In a medium bowl, mix the egg, mozzarella cheese, pizza sauce, and almond flour.
3. Open the iron and add a quarter of the mixture. Close and cook until crispy, 5 minutes.
4. Open the lid, sprinkle with a little more of the mozzarella cheese, and a pepperoni slice. Close the lid and cook further for 2 minutes.
5. Transfer the chaffle to a plate and make 3 more chaffles in the same manner.
6. Serve afterward.

**Nutrition Facts per Serving**

Calories 60 | Fats 4.41g | Carbs 1.24g | Net Carbs 0.94g | Protein 3.74g

# Tuna Melt Chaffles

Prep time: 12 minutes | Cook time: 35 minutes | Serves: 4

## Ingredients:

### For the chaffles:

- 2 eggs, beaten
- 1 cup finely grated mozzarella cheese
- Salt and freshly ground black pepper to taste

- 1 celery stalk, chopped
- 2 shallots, finely chopped
- 2 tbsp mayonnaise
- ½ tbsp relish
- Salt and freshly ground black pepper to taste
- 2 sliced cheddar cheese

### For the tuna filling:

- 2 (5 oz) cans tuna in water, drained

## Instructions:

### For the chaffles:

1. Preheat the waffle iron.
2. In a medium bowl, mix the egg, mozzarella cheese, salt, and black pepper.
3. Open the iron and add a quarter of the mixture. Close and cook until crispy, 7 minutes.
4. Transfer the chaffle to a plate and make 3 more chaffles in the same manner.

### For the tuna salad:

5. In a medium bowl, mix the tuna, celery, shallots, mayonnaise, relish, salt, and black pepper.
6. Divide the tuna mixture on two chaffles, top with a cheddar slice each and cover with the remaining pieces of chaffles.
7. Place the sandwich in an oven and bake until the cheese melts, 5 to 7 minutes.
8. Remove from the oven and serve afterward.

## Nutrition Facts per Serving

Calories 102 | Fats 4.5g | Carbs 3g | Net Carbs 2.2g | Protein 12.33g

# Grilled Cheese Sandwich Chaffles

Prep time: 10 minutes | Cook time: 28 minutes | Serves: 4

## Ingredients:

- 1 egg, beaten
- 1 cup finely grated cheddar cheese
- 10 slices Swiss cheese

## Instructions:

1. Preheat the waffle iron.
2. In a medium bowl, mix the egg and cheddar cheese.
3. Open the iron and add a quarter of the mixture. Close and cook until crispy, 5 minutes.
4. Put the chaffle on a plate and make 3 more.
5. Allow cooling and cut the chaffles into quarters.
6. Sandwich one Swiss cheese slice between two chaffles and repeat until the cheese slices are all sandwiched.
7. Return the chaffles to the waffle iron, four sets at a time and cook further for 2 minutes or until the cheese melts.
8. Remove, put on a plate and serve afterward.

## Nutrition Facts per Serving

Calories 432 | Fats 33.03g | Carbs 4.46g | Net Carbs 4.46g | Protein 29.03g

# Buffalo Chicken Chaffles

Prep time: 10 minutes | Cook time: 28 minutes | Serves: 4

## Ingredients:

- 2 eggs, beaten
- 2 tbsp hot sauce
- 1 cup finely grated cheddar cheese
- 2 tbsp cream cheese
- 1/3 cup cooked chicken, diced

## Instructions:

1. Preheat the waffle iron.
2. In a medium bowl, mix the eggs, hot sauce, cheddar cheese, and cream cheese until well combined. Add the chicken and fold in well.
3. Open the iron and add a quarter of the mixture. Close and cook until crispy, 5 minutes.
4. Open the lid, flip the chaffle and cook further for 2 minutes.
5. Transfer the chaffle to a plate and make 3 more chaffles in the same manner.
6. Serve afterward.

## Nutrition Facts per Serving

Calories 232 | Fats 19.18g | Carbs 1.46g | Net Carbs 1.26g | Protein 13.25g

# Chicken Pancetta Ranch Chaffles

Prep time: 10 minutes | Cook time: 14 minutes | Serves: 2

## Ingredients:

- 1 egg, beaten
- 1 piece pancetta, cooked and chopped
- 1/3 cup finely grated Monterey Jack cheese
- 1 tsp powdered ranch dressing
- 1/3 cup cooked chicken, diced

## Instructions:

1. Preheat the waffle iron.
2. In a medium bowl, mix the egg, pancetta, Monterey Jack cheese, and ranch dressing until well combined. Add the chicken and fold in well.
3. Open the iron and add half of the mixture. Close and cook until crispy, 5 minutes.
4. Open the lid, flip the chaffle and cook further for 2 minutes.
5. Transfer the chaffle to a plate and make another chaffle in the same manner.
6. Serve afterward.

## Nutrition Facts per Serving

Calories 371 | Fats 26.01g | Carbs 0.45g | Net Carbs 0.45g | Protein 32g

# Bacon Cheeseburger Chaffles

Prep time: 10 minutes | Cook time: 28 minutes | Serves: 4

## Ingredients:

- ½ cup cooked ground beef
- 2 eggs, beaten
- 2 tsp steak seasoning
- ½ cup finely grated cheddar cheese
- ½ cup finely grated mozzarella cheese
- 3 bacon slices, cooked and crumbled

## Instructions:

1. Preheat the waffle iron.
2. Add all the ingredients to a large bowl and mix well.
3. Open the iron and add a quarter of the mixture. Close and cook until crispy, 5 minutes.
4. Open the lid, flip the chaffle and cook further for 2 minutes.
5. Transfer the chaffle to a plate and make 3 more chaffles in the same manner.
6. Serve afterward.

## Nutrition Facts per Serving

Calories 332 | Fats 23.78g | Carbs 2.11g | Net Carbs 1.81g | Protein 25.89g

# Mini Chaffles and Crispy Chicken Meatballs

Prep time: 15 minutes | Cook time: 31 minutes | Serves: 4

## Ingredients:

### For the chicken meatballs:

- 1 lb ground chicken
- 1 tsp sugar-free maple syrup
- 1/4 tsp cayenne pepper
- 1 large egg
- 1/3 cup pork rinds
- Salt and freshly ground black pepper to taste
- ¼ cup olive oil
- 2 scallions, chopped

### For the chaffles:

- 2 large eggs, beaten
- 1 cup finely grated cheddar cheese

## Instructions:

### For the chicken meatballs:

1. Preheat an oven to 400 F and line a baking sheet with parchment paper.
2. In a large bowl, mix the chicken, maple syrup, cayenne pepper, egg, pork rinds, salt, and black pepper. Form 1-inch balls out of the mixture and set aside.
3. Heat the olive oil in a medium skillet and fry the meatballs until brown on the outside, 3 minutes.
4. Transfer the meatballs to the baking sheet and bake further for 10 to 12 minutes or until cooked through and brown.
5. Take out of the oven and set aside for serving.

### For the chaffles:

7. Meanwhile, preheat the waffle iron.
8. Mix the eggs and cheese in a medium bowl.
9. Open the iron and add a quarter of the mixture. Close and cook until crispy, 7 minutes.
10. Transfer the chaffle to a plate and make 3 more chaffles in the same manner.
11. Divide the chaffles into quarters, top with the meatballs, garnish the scallions and serve.

## Nutrition Facts per Serving

Calories 571 | Fats 45.95g | Carbs 1.38g | Net Carbs 1.18g | Protein 36.71g

# Smoked Salmon and Dill Waffles

Prep time: 10 minutes | Cook time: 28 minutes | Serves: 4

## Ingredients:

- 2 eggs, beaten
- 1/3 cup cream cheese, softened
- 1 cup finely grated Gouda cheese
- Salt and freshly ground black pepper to taste
- 2 tbsp chopped fresh dill + extra for garnishing
- ½ cup smoked salmon, chopped

## Instructions:

1. Preheat the waffle iron.
2. In a medium bowl, mix the eggs, cream cheese, Gouda cheese, salt, black pepper, dill, and salmon.
3. Open the iron and add a quarter of the mixture. Close and cook until crispy, 7 minutes.
4. Transfer the chaffle to a plate and make 3 more chaffles in the same manner.
5. Divide the chaffles into quarters, garnish with some dill and serve afterward.

## Nutrition Facts per Serving

Calories 238 | Fats 18.11g | Carbs 3.22g | Net Carbs 2.52g | Protein 16.05g

# French Onion Soup Chaffles

Prep time: 10 minutes | Cook time: 28 minutes | Serves: 4

## Ingredients:

- 2 eggs, beaten
- 1 cup finely grated Gruyere cheese
- 1/3 cup cream cheese, softened
- ¼ cup caramelized onions
- Salt and freshly ground black pepper to taste
- 1/6 tsp dried thyme
- 2 tbsp chopped fresh chives to garnish

## Instructions:

1. Preheat the waffle iron.
2. In a medium bowl, mix all the ingredients except the chives.
3. Open the iron and add a quarter of the mixture. Close and cook until crispy, 7 minutes.
4. Transfer the chaffle to a plate and make 3 more chaffles in the same manner.
5. Garnish the chaffles with the chives and serve afterward.

## Nutrition Facts per Serving

Calories 230 | Fats 18.45g | Carbs 1.71g | Net Carbs 1.51g | Protein 14.14g

# Prosciutto and Avocado Chaffles

Prep time: 10 minutes | Cook time: 28 minutes | Serves: 4

**Ingredients:**

- 2 eggs, beaten
- 3 prosciutto slices, cooked and chopped
- 2 avocados, pitted and pulp mashed
- 1 cup finely grated cheddar cheese

**Instructions:**

1. Preheat the waffle iron.
2. In a medium bowl, mix all the ingredients.
3. Open the iron and add a quarter of the mixture. Close and cook until crispy, 7 minutes.
4. Transfer the chaffle to a plate and make 3 more chaffles in the same manner.
5. Allow cooling and serve the chaffles afterward.

**Nutrition Facts per Serving**

Calories 346 | Fats 29.15g | Carbs 9.64g | Net Carbs 2.94g | Protein 14.57g

# Sloppy Joe Chaffles

Prep time: 15 minutes | Cook time: 35 minutes | Serves: 4

## Ingredients:

### For the meat topping:

- 1 lb ground beef
- ½ medium red onion, chopped
- 2 garlic cloves, minced
- Salt and freshly ground black pepper to taste
- 3 tbsp tomato paste
- 1 tsp cayenne pepper
- 1 tsp unsweetened cocoa powder
- ½ cup chicken broth
- 1 tsp coconut aminos
- 1 tsp mustard powder
- 1 tsp erythritol
- ½ tsp smoked paprika
- 2 tbsp chopped fresh scallions for garnishing

### For the chaffles:

- 2 eggs, beaten
- 1 cup finely grated cheddar cheese

## Instructions:

### For the meat topping:

1. Put the beef, onion, garlic, salt, and black pepper in a medium pot and cook over medium heat until no longer pink, 5 minutes.
2. Stir in the tomato paste, cayenne pepper, cocoa powder, and cook for 2 minutes.
3. Mix in the chicken broth, coconut aminos, mustard powder, erythritol, and paprika. Allow boiling and reduce the heat to low. Simmer for 20 minutes.
4. Turn the heat off when ready and adjust the taste with salt and black pepper.

### For the chaffles:

5. Meanwhile, preheat the waffle iron.
6. In a medium bowl, mix the eggs and cheddar cheese.
7. Open the iron and add a quarter of the mixture. Close and cook until crispy, 7 minutes.
8. Transfer the chaffle to a plate and make 3 more chaffles in the same manner.
9. To serve, top the chaffles with the meat, garnish with the scallions and enjoy.

## Nutrition Facts per Serving

Calories 466 | Fats 28.94g | Carbs 6.15g | Net Carbs 4.85g | Protein 43.86g

# Asian Cauliflower Chaffles

Prep time: 20 minutes | Cook time: 28 minutes | Serves: 4

## Ingredients:

### For the chaffles:

- 1 cup cauliflower rice, steamed
- 1 large egg, beaten
- Salt and freshly ground black pepper to taste
- 1 cup finely grated Parmesan cheese
- 1 tsp sesame seeds
- ¼ cup chopped fresh scallions

### For the dipping sauce:

- 3 tbsp coconut aminos
- 1 ½ tbsp plain vinegar
- 1 tsp fresh ginger puree
- 1 tsp fresh garlic paste
- 3 tbsp sesame oil
- 1 tsp fish sauce
- 1 tsp red chili flakes

## Instructions:

1. Preheat the waffle iron.
2. In a medium bowl, mix the cauliflower rice, egg, salt, black pepper, and Parmesan cheese.
3. Open the iron and add a quarter of the mixture. Close and cook until crispy, 7 minutes.
4. Transfer the chaffle to a plate and make 3 more chaffles in the same manner.
Meanwhile, make the dipping sauce.
5. In a medium bowl, mix all the ingredients for the dipping sauce.
6. Plate the chaffles, garnish with the sesame seeds and scallions and serve with the dipping sauce.

## Nutrition Facts per Serving

Calories 231 | Fats 18.88g | Carbs 6.32g | Net Carbs 5.42g | Protein 9.66g

# Hot Dog Chaffles

Prep time: 15 minutes | Cook time: 14 minutes | Serves: 2

## Ingredients:

- 1 egg, beaten
- 1 cup finely grated cheddar cheese
- 2 hot dog sausages, cooked
- Mustard dressing for topping
- 8 pickle slices

## Instructions:

1. Preheat the waffle iron.
2. In a medium bowl, mix the egg and cheddar cheese.
3. Open the iron and add half of the mixture. Close and cook until crispy, 7 minutes.
4. Transfer the chaffle to a plate and make a second chaffle in the same manner.
5. To serve, top each chaffle with a sausage, swirl the mustard dressing on top, and then divide the pickle slices on top.
6. Enjoy!

## Nutrition Facts per Serving

Calories 231 | Fats 18.29g | Carbs 2.8g | Net Carbs 2.6g | Protein 13.39g

# Spicy Shrimp and Chaffles

Prep time: 15 minutes | Cook time: 31 minutes | Serves: 4

## Ingredients:

### For the shrimp:
- 1 tbsp olive oil
- 1 lb jumbo shrimp, peeled and deveined
- 1 tbsp Creole seasoning
- Salt to taste
- 2 tbsp hot sauce
- 3 tbsp butter
- 2 tbsp chopped fresh scallions to garnish

### For the chaffles:
- 2 eggs, beaten
- 1 cup finely grated Monterey Jack cheese

## Instructions:

### For the shrimp:
1. Heat the olive oil in a medium skillet over medium heat.
2. Season the shrimp with the Creole seasoning and salt. Cook in the oil until pink and opaque on both sides, 2 minutes.
3. Pour in the hot sauce and butter. Mix well until the shrimp is adequately coated in the sauce, 1 minute.
4. Turn the heat off and set aside.

### For the chaffles:
7. Preheat the waffle iron.
8. In a medium bowl, mix the eggs and Monterey Jack cheese.
9. Open the iron and add a quarter of the mixture. Close and cook until crispy, 7 minutes.
10. Transfer the chaffle to a plate and make 3 more chaffles in the same manner.
11. Cut the chaffles into quarters and place on a plate.
12. Top with the shrimp and garnish with the scallions.
13. Serve warm.

## Nutrition Facts per Serving
Calories 342 | Fats 19.75g | Carbs 2.8g | Net Carbs 2.3g | Protein 36.01g

# Chicken Jalapeño Chaffles

Prep time: 15 minutes | Cook time: 14 minutes | Serves: 2

## Ingredients:

- 1/8 cup finely grated Parmesan cheese
- ¼ cup finely grated cheddar cheese
- 1 egg, beaten
- ½ cup cooked chicken breasts, diced
- 1 small jalapeño pepper, deseeded and minced
- 1/8 tsp garlic powder
- 1/8 tsp onion powder
- 1 tsp cream cheese, softened

## Instructions:

1. Preheat the waffle iron.
2. In a medium bowl, mix all the ingredients until adequately combined.
3. Open the iron and add half of the mixture. Close and cook until crispy, 7 minutes.
4. Transfer the chaffle to a plate and make a second chaffle in the same manner.
5. Allow cooling and serve afterward.

## Nutrition Facts per Serving

Calories 201 | Fats 11.49g | Carbs 3.76g | Net Carbs 3.36g | Protein 20.11g

# Chicken and Chaffle Nachos

Prep time: 15 minutes | Cook time: 33 minutes | Serves: 4

## Ingredients:

### For the chaffles:

- 2 eggs, beaten
- 1 cup finely grated Mexican cheese blend

### For the chicken-cheese topping:

- 2 tbsp butter
- 1 tbsp almond flour
- ¼ cup unsweetened almond milk

- 1 cup finely grated cheddar cheese + more to garnish
- 3 bacon slices, cooked and chopped
- 2 cups cooked and diced chicken breasts
- 2 tbsp hot sauce
- 2 tbsp chopped fresh scallions

## Instructions:

### For the chaffles:

1. Preheat the waffle iron.
2. In a medium bowl, mix the eggs and Mexican cheese blend.
3. Open the iron and add a quarter of the mixture. Close and cook until crispy, 7 minutes.
4. Transfer the chaffle to a plate and make 3 more chaffles in the same manner.
5. Place the chaffles on serving plates and set aside for serving.

### For the chicken-cheese topping:

6. Melt the butter in a large skillet and mix in the almond flour until brown, 1 minute.
7. Pour the almond milk and whisk until well combined. Simmer until thickened, 2 minutes.
8. Stir in the cheese to melt, 2 minutes and then mix in the bacon, chicken, and hot sauce.
9. Spoon the mixture onto the chaffles and top with some more cheddar cheese.
10. Garnish with the scallions and serve immediately.

## Nutrition Facts per Serving

Calories 524 | Fats 37.51g | Carbs 3.55g | Net Carbs 3.25g | Protein 41.86g

# Buffalo Hummus Beef Chaffles

Prep time: 15 minutes | Cook time: 32 minutes | Serves: 4

## Ingredients:

- 2 eggs
- 1 cup + ¼ cup finely grated cheddar cheese, divided
- 2 chopped fresh scallions
- Salt and freshly ground black pepper to taste
- 2 chicken breasts, cooked and diced
- ¼ cup buffalo sauce
- 3 tbsp low-carb hummus
- 2 celery stalks, chopped
- ¼ cup crumbled blue cheese for topping

## Instructions:

1. Preheat the waffle iron.
2. In a medium bowl, mix the eggs, 1 cup of the cheddar cheese, scallions, salt, and black pepper,
3. Open the iron and add a quarter of the mixture. Close and cook until crispy, 7 minutes.
4. Transfer the chaffle to a plate and make 3 more chaffles in the same manner.
5. Preheat the oven to 400 F and line a baking sheet with parchment paper. Set aside.
6. Cut the chaffles into quarters and arrange on the baking sheet.
7. In a medium bowl, mix the chicken with the buffalo sauce, hummus, and celery.
8. Spoon the chicken mixture onto each quarter of chaffles and top with the remaining cheddar cheese.
9. Place the baking sheet in the oven and bake until the cheese melts, 4 minutes.
10. Remove from the oven and top with the blue cheese.
11. Serve afterward.

## Nutrition Facts per Serving

Calories 552 | Fats 28.37g | Carbs 6.97g | Net Carbs 6.07g | Protein 59.8g

# Pulled Pork Chaffle Sandwiches

Prep time: 20 minutes | Cook time: 28 minutes | Serves: 4

## Ingredients:

- 2 eggs, beaten
- 1 cup finely grated cheddar cheese
- ¼ tsp baking powder
- 2 cups cooked and shredded pork
- 1 tbsp sugar-free BBQ sauce
- 2 cups shredded coleslaw mix
- 2 tbsp apple cider vinegar
- ½ tsp salt
- ¼ cup ranch dressing

## Instructions:

1. Preheat the waffle iron.
2. In a medium bowl, mix the eggs, cheddar cheese, and baking powder.
3. Open the iron and add a quarter of the mixture. Close and cook until crispy, 7 minutes.
4. Transfer the chaffle to a plate and make 3 more chaffles in the same manner.
5. Meanwhile, in another medium bowl, mix the pulled pork with the BBQ sauce until well combined. Set aside.
6. Also, mix the coleslaw mix, apple cider vinegar, salt, and ranch dressing in another medium bowl.
7. When the chaffles are ready, on two pieces, divide the pork and then top with the ranch coleslaw. Cover with the remaining chaffles and insert mini skewers to secure the sandwiches.
8. Enjoy afterward.

## Nutrition Facts per Serving

Calories 374 | Fats 23.61g | Carbs 8.2g | Net Carbs 8.2g | Protein 28.05g

# Okonomiyaki Chaffles

Prep time: 20 minutes | Cook time: 28 minutes | Serves: 4

## Ingredients:

### For the chaffles:

- 2 eggs, beaten
- 1 cup finely grated mozzarella cheese
- ½ tsp baking powder
- ¼ cup shredded radishes

### For the sauce:

- 2 tsp coconut aminos
- 2 tbsp sugar-free ketchup

- 1 tbsp sugar-free maple syrup
- 2 tsp Worcestershire sauce

### For the topping:

- 1 tbsp mayonnaise
- 2 tbsp chopped fresh scallions
- 2 tbsp bonito flakes
- 1 tsp dried seaweed powder
- 1 tbsp pickled ginger

## Instructions:

### For the chaffles:

1. Preheat the waffle iron.
2. In a medium bowl, mix the eggs, mozzarella cheese, baking powder, and radishes.
3. Open the iron and add a quarter of the mixture. Close and cook until crispy, 7 minutes.
4. Transfer the chaffle to a plate and make a 3 more chaffles in the same manner.

### For the sauce:

5. Combine the coconut aminos, ketchup, maple syrup, and Worcestershire sauce in a medium bowl and mix well.

### For the topping:

6. In another mixing bowl, mix the mayonnaise, scallions, bonito flakes, seaweed powder, and ginger

### To serve:

7. Arrange the chaffles on four different plates and swirl the sauce on top. Spread the topping on the chaffles and serve afterward.

## Nutrition Facts per Serving

Calories 90 | Fats 3.32g | Carbs 2.97g | Net Carbs 2.17g | Protein 12.09g

# Keto Reuben Chaffles

Prep time: 15 minutes | Cook time: 28 minutes | Serves: 4

## Ingredients:

### For the chaffles:
- 2 eggs, beaten
- 1 cup finely grated Swiss cheese
- 2 tsp caraway seeds
- 1/8 tsp salt
- ½ tsp baking powder

### For the sauce:
- 2 tbsp sugar-free ketchup
- 3 tbsp mayonnaise
- 1 tbsp dill relish
- 1 tsp hot sauce

### For the filling:
- 6 oz pastrami
- 2 Swiss cheese slices
- ¼ cup pickled radishes

## Instructions:

### For the chaffles:
1. Preheat the waffle iron.
2. In a medium bowl, mix the eggs, Swiss cheese, caraway seeds, salt, and baking powder.
3. Open the iron and add a quarter of the mixture. Close and cook until crispy, 7 minutes.
4. Transfer the chaffle to a plate and make 3 more chaffles in the same manner.

### For the sauce:
5. In another bowl, mix the ketchup, mayonnaise, dill relish, and hot sauce.

### To assemble:
6. Divide on two chaffles; the sauce, the pastrami, Swiss cheese slices, and pickled radishes.
7. Cover with the other chaffles, divide the sandwich in halves and serve.

## Nutrition Facts per Serving
Calories 316 | Fats 21.78g | Carbs 6.52g | Net Carbs 5.42g | Protein 23.56g

Dessert Chaffles

# Chapter 7 Dessert

## Pumpkin Cake Chaffle with Cream Cheese Frosting

Prep time: 15 minutes | Cook time: 28 minutes | Serves: 4

### Ingredients:

*For the pumpkin chaffles:*

- 2 eggs, beaten
- ½ tsp pumpkin pie spice
- 1 cup finely grated mozzarella cheese
- 1 tbsp pumpkin puree

*For the cream cheese frosting:*

- 2 tbsp cream cheese, softened
- 2 tbsp swerve confectioner's sugar
- ½ tsp vanilla extract

### Instructions:

*For the chaffles:*

1. Preheat the waffle iron.
2. In a medium bowl, mix the egg, pumpkin pie spice, mozzarella cheese, and pumpkin puree.
3. Open the iron and add a quarter of the mixture. Close and cook until crispy, 7 minutes.
4. Transfer the chaffle to a plate and make 3 more chaffles with the remaining batter.

*For the cream cheese frosting:*

5. Add the cream cheese, swerve sugar, and vanilla to a medium bowl and whisk using an electric mixer until smooth and fluffy.
6. Layer the chaffles one on another but with some frosting spread between the layers. Top with the bit of frosting.
7. Slice and serve.

### Nutrition Facts per Serving

Calories 106 | Fats 5.17g | Carbs 1.9g | Net Carbs 1.2g | Protein 12.82g

# Birthday Cake Chaffles

Prep time: 15 minutes | Cook time: 28 minutes | Serves: 4

## Ingredients:

### For the chaffles:
- 2 eggs, beaten
- 1 cup finely grated Swiss cheese

### For the frosting and topping:
- ½ cup heavy cream
- 2 tbsp sugar-free maple syrup
- ½ tsp vanilla extract
- 3 tbsp funfetti

## Instructions:

### For the chaffles:
1. Preheat the waffle iron.
2. In a medium bowl, mix the egg and Swiss cheese.
3. Open the iron and add a quarter of the mixture. Close and cook until crispy, 7 minutes.
4. Transfer the chaffle to a plate and make 3 more chaffles with the remaining batter.

### For the frosting and topping:
8. Add the heavy cream, maple syrup, and vanilla extract in a medium bowl and whisk using an electric mixer until smooth and fluffy.
9. Layer the chaffles one on another but with some frosting spread between the layers.
10. Top with the remaining bit of frosting and garnish with the funfetti.

## Nutrition Facts per Serving

Calories 210 | Fats 16.82g | Carbs 2.42g | Net Carbs 2.42g | Protein 11.96g

# S'mores Chaffles

Prep time: 15 minutes | Cook time: 28 minutes | Serves: 4

## Ingredients:

- 2 eggs, beaten
- 1 cup finely grated Gruyere cheese
- ½ tsp vanilla extract
- 2 tbsp swerve brown sugar
- A pinch of salt
- ¼ cup unsweetened chocolate chips, melted
- 2 tbsp low carb marshmallow fluff

## Instructions:

1. Preheat the waffle iron.
2. In a medium bowl, mix the eggs, Gruyere cheese, vanilla, swerve sugar, and salt.
3. Open the iron and add a quarter of the mixture. Close and cook until crispy, 7 minutes.
4. Transfer the chaffle to a plate and make 3 more chaffles with the remaining batter.
5. Spread half of the chocolate on two chaffles, add the marshmallow fluff and cover with the other chaffles.
6. Swirl the remaining chocolate, slice in half and serve.

## Nutrition Facts per Serving

Calories 203 | Fats 15.49g | Carbs 0.95g | Net Carbs 0.95g | Protein 14.32g

# Chocolate Cake Chaffles with Cream Cheese Frosting

Prep time: 10 minutes | Cook time: 28 minutes | Serves: 4

## Ingredients:

### *For the chaffles:*

- 2 eggs, beaten
- 1 cup finely grated Gouda cheese
- 2 tsp unsweetened cocoa powder
- ¼ tsp sugar-free maple syrup
- 1 tbsp cream cheese, softened

### *For the frosting:*

- 3 tbsp cream cheese, softened
- ¼ tsp vanilla extract
- 2 tbsp sugar-free maple syrup

## Instructions:

### *For the chaffles:*

1. Preheat the waffle iron.
2. In a medium bowl, mix all the ingredients for the chaffles.
3. Open the iron and add a quarter of the mixture. Close and cook until crispy, 7 minutes.
4. Transfer the chaffle to a plate and make 3 more chaffles with the remaining batter.

### *For the frosting:*

5. In a medium bowl, beat the cream cheese, vanilla extract, and maple syrup with a hand mixer until smooth.
6. Assemble the chaffles with the frosting to make the cake making sure to top the last layer with some frosting.
7. Slice and serve.

## Nutrition Facts per Serving

Calories 78 | Fats 6.5g | Carbs 1.24g | Net Carbs 0.94g | Protein 3.99g

# Lemon Cake Chaffle with Lemon Frosting

Prep time: 10 minutes | Cook time: 28 minutes | Serves: 4

## Ingredients:

### For the chaffles:

- 2 eggs, beaten
- ½ cup finely grated Swiss cheese
- 2 oz cream cheese, softened
- ½ tsp lemon extract
- 20 drops cake batter extract

### For the frosting:

- ½ cup heavy cream
- 1 tbsp sugar-free maple syrup
- ¼ tsp lemon extract

## Instructions:

### For the chaffles:

1. Preheat the waffle iron.
2. In a medium bowl, mix all the ingredients for the chaffles.
3. Open the iron and add a quarter of the mixture. Close and cook until crispy, 7 minutes.
4. Transfer the chaffle to a plate and make 3 more chaffles with the remaining batter.

### For the frosting:

5. In a medium bowl, using a hand mixer, beat the heavy cream, maple syrup, and lemon extract until fluffy.
6. Assemble the chaffles with the frosting to make the cake.
7. Slice and serve.

## Nutrition Facts per Serving

Calories 176 | Fats 15.18g | Carbs 2.88g | Net Carbs 2.88g | Protein 7.63g

# Red Velvet Chaffle Cake

Prep time: 15 minutes | Cook time: 28 minutes | Serves: 4

## Ingredients:

### For the chaffles:

- 2 eggs, beaten
- ½ cup finely grated Parmesan cheese
- 2 oz cream cheese, softened
- 2 drops red food coloring
- 1 tsp vanilla extract

### For the frosting:

- 3 tbsp cream cheese, softened
- 1 tbsp sugar-free maple syrup
- ¼ tsp vanilla extract

## Instructions:

### For the chaffles:

1. Preheat the waffle iron.
2. In a medium bowl, mix all the ingredients for the chaffles.
3. Open the iron and add a quarter of the mixture. Close and cook until crispy, 7 minutes.
4. Transfer the chaffle to a plate and make 3 more chaffles with the remaining batter.

### For the frosting:

5. In a medium bowl, using a hand mixer, whisk the cream cheese, maple syrup, and vanilla extract until smooth.
6. Assemble the chaffles with the frosting to make the cake.
7. Slice and serve.

## Nutrition Facts per Serving

Calories 147 | Fats 9.86g | Carbs 5.22g | Net Carbs 5.22g | Protein 8.57g

# Almond Butter Chaffle Cake with Chocolate Butter Frosting

Prep time: 20 minutes | Cook time: 28 minutes | Serves: 4

## Ingredients:

### *For the chaffles:*

- 1 egg, beaten
- ⅓ cup finely grated mozzarella cheese
- 1 tbsp almond flour
- 2 tbsp almond butter
- 1 tbsp swerve confectioner's sugar
- ½ tsp vanilla extract

### *For the chocolate butter frosting:*

- 1½ cups butter, room temperature
- 1 cup unsweetened cocoa powder
- ½ cup almond milk
- 5 cups swerve confectioner's sugar
- 2 tsp vanilla extract

## Instructions:

### *For the chaffles:*

1. Preheat the waffle iron.
2. In a medium bowl, mix the egg, mozzarella cheese, almond flour, almond butter, swerve confectioner's sugar, and vanilla extract.
3. Open the iron and add a quarter of the mixture. Close and cook until crispy, 7 minutes.
4. Transfer the chaffle to a plate and make 3 more chaffles with the remaining batter.

### *For the frosting:*

5. In a medium bowl, cream the butter and cocoa powder until smooth.
6. Gradually, whisk in the almond milk and swerve confectioner's sugar until smooth.
7. Add the vanilla extract and mix well.
8. Assemble the chaffles with the frosting to make the cake.
9. Slice and serve.

## Nutrition Facts per Serving

Calories 838 | Fats 85.35g | Carbs 8.73g | Net Carbs 2.03g | Protein 13.59g

# Cinnamon Chaffles with Custard Filling

Prep time: 25 minutes | Cook time: 28 minutes | Serves: 4

## Ingredients:

### For the custard filling:
- 4 egg yolks, beaten
- 1 tbsp erythritol
- ¼ tsp xanthan gum
- 1 cup heavy cream
- 1 tbsp vanilla extract

### For the chaffles:
- 2 eggs, beaten

- 2 tbsp cream cheese, softened
- 1 cup finely grated Monterey Jack cheese
- 1 tsp vanilla extract
- 1 tbsp heavy cream
- 1 tbsp coconut flour
- ½ tsp baking powder
- ½ tsp ground cinnamon
- ¼ tsp erythritol

## Instructions:

### For the custard filling:
1. In a medium bowl, beat the egg yolks with the erythritol. Mix in the xanthan gum until smooth.
2. Pour the heavy cream into a medium saucepan and simmer over low heat. Pour the mixture into the egg mixture while whisking vigorously until well mixed.
3. Transfer the mixture to the saucepan and continue whisking while cooking over low heat until thickened, 20 to 30 seconds. Turn the heat off and stir in the vanilla extract.
4. Strain the custard through a fine-mesh into a bowl. Cover the bowl with plastic wrap.
5. Refrigerate for 1 hour.

### For the chaffles:
6. After 1 hour, preheat the waffle iron.
7. In a medium bowl, mix all the ingredients for the chaffles.
8. Open the iron and add a quarter of the mixture. Close and cook until crispy, 7 minutes.
9. Transfer the chaffle to a plate and make 3 more with the remaining batter.

### To serve:
10. Spread the custard filling between two chaffle quarters, sandwich and enjoy!

## Nutrition Facts per Serving

Calories 239 | Fats 21.25g | Carbs 3.21g | Net Carbs 3.01g | Protein 6.73g

# Tiramisu Chaffles

Prep time: 20 minutes | Cook time: 28 minutes | Serves: 4

## Ingredients:

### For the chaffles:
- 2 eggs, beaten
- 3 tbsp cream cheese, softened
- ½ cup finely grated Gouda cheese
- 1 tsp vanilla extract
- 1/4 tsp erythritol

### For the coffee syrup:
- 2 tbsp strong coffee, room temperature
- 3 tbsp sugar-free maple syrup

### For the filling:
- ¼ cup heavy cream
- 2 tsp vanilla extract
- ¼ tsp erythritol
- 4 tbsp mascarpone cheese, room temperature
- 1 tbsp cream cheese, softened

### For dusting:
- ½ tsp unsweetened cocoa powder

## Instructions:

### For the chaffles:
1. Preheat the waffle iron.
2. In a medium bowl, mix all the ingredients for the chaffles.
3. Open the iron and add a quarter of the mixture. Close and cook until crispy, 7 minutes.
4. Transfer the chaffle to a plate and make 3 more with the remaining batter.

### For the coffee syrup:
5. In a small bowl, mix the coffee and maple syrup. Set aside.

### For the filling:

6. Beat the heavy cream, vanilla, and erythritol in a medium bowl using an electric hand mixer until stiff peak forms.
7. In another bowl, beat the mascarpone cheese and cream cheese until well combined. Add the heavy cream mixture and fold in. Spoon the mixture into a piping bag.

### To assemble:

8. Spoon 1 tbsp of the coffee syrup on one chaffle and pipe some of the cream cheese mixture on top. Cover with another chaffle and continue the assembling process.
9. Generously dust with cocoa powder and refrigerate overnight.
10. When ready to enjoy, slice and serve.

## Nutrition Facts per Serving

Calories 208 | Fats 15.91g | Carbs 4.49g | Net Carbs 4.39g | Protein 10.1g

# Coconut Chaffles with Mint Frosting

Prep time: 15 minutes | Cook time: 28 minutes | Serves: 4

## Ingredients:

### For the chaffles:

- 2 eggs, beaten
- 2 tbsp cream cheese, softened
- 1 cup finely grated Monterey Jack cheese
- 2 tbsp coconut flour
- ¼ tsp baking powder
- 1 tbsp unsweetened shredded coconut
- 1 tbsp walnuts, chopped

### For the frosting:

- ¼ cup unsalted butter, room temperature
- 3 tbsp almond milk
- 1 tsp mint extract
- 2 drops green food coloring
- 3 cups swerve confectioner's sugar

## Instructions:

### For the chaffles:

1. Preheat the waffle iron.
2. In a medium bowl, mix all the ingredients for the chaffles.
3. Open the iron and add a quarter of the mixture. Close and cook until crispy, 7 minutes.
4. Transfer the chaffle to a plate and make 3 more with the remaining batter.

### For the frosting:

5. In a medium bowl, cream the butter using an electric hand mixer until smooth.
6. Gradually mix in the almond milk until smooth.
7. Add the mint extract and green food coloring; whisk until well combined.
8. Finally, mix in the swerve confectioner's sugar a cup at a time until smooth.
9. Layer the chaffles with the frosting.
10. Slice and serve afterward.

## Nutrition Facts per Serving

Calories 141 | Fats 13.13g | Carbs 1.31g | Net Carbs 1.03g | Protein 4.31g

# Cinnamon Roll Chaffles

Prep time: 15 minutes | Cook time: 28 minutes | Serves: 4

## Ingredients:

### For the cinnamon roll chaffles:
- ½ cup finely grated mozzarella cheese
- 1 egg, beaten
- 1 tsp cinnamon powder
- 1 tbsp almond flour
- 1 tsp erythritol

### For the cinnamon roll swirl:
- 1 tbsp butter
- 1 tsp cinnamon powder
- 2 tsp erythritol

### For the cinnamon roll glaze:
- 1 tbsp butter, melted
- 1 tbsp cream cheese, melted
- ¼ tsp vanilla extract
- 2 tsp swerve confectioner's sugar

## Instructions:
1. Preheat the waffle iron.
2. In a medium bowl, mix all the ingredients for the chaffles. Set aside.
3. In another bowl, mix all the ingredients for the cinnamon roll swirl.
4. Open the iron and lightly grease with cooking spray. Add a quarter of the chaffle mixture and top with the cinnamon roll swirl mixture.
5. Close the lid and cook until brown and crispy, 7 minutes.
6. Transfer the chaffle to a plate and make 3 more with the remaining ingredients.
7. Meanwhile, in a small bowl, whisk the glaze ingredients until smooth.
8. Drizzle the glaze over the chaffles when they are ready and serve afterward.

## Nutrition Facts per Serving
Calories 112 | Fats 10.2g | Carbs 2.1g | Net Carbs 1.2g | Protein 3.38g

# Chocolate Melt Chaffles

Prep time: 15 minutes | Cook time: 36 minutes | Serves: 4

## Ingredients

### For the chaffles:
- 2 eggs, beaten
- ¼ cup finely grated Gruyere cheese
- 2 tbsp heavy cream
- 1 tbsp coconut flour
- 2 tbsp cream cheese, softened
- 3 tbsp unsweetened cocoa powder
- 2 tsp vanilla extract
- A pinch of salt

### For the chocolate sauce:
- 1/3 cup + 1 tbsp heavy cream
- 1 ½ oz unsweetened baking chocolate, chopped
- 1 ½ tsp sugar-free maple syrup
- 1 ½ tsp vanilla extract

## Instructions:

### For the chaffles:
1. Preheat the waffle iron.
2. In a medium bowl, mix all the ingredients for the chaffles.
3. Open the iron and add a quarter of the mixture. Close and cook until crispy, 7 minutes.
4. Transfer the chaffle to a plate and make 3 more with the remaining batter.

### For the chocolate sauce:
5. Pour the heavy cream into saucepan and simmer over low heat, 3 minutes.
6. Turn the heat off and add the chocolate. Allow melting for a few minutes and stir until fully melted, 5 minutes.
7. Mix in the maple syrup and vanilla extract.
8. Assemble the chaffles in layers with the chocolate sauce sandwiched between each layer.
9. Slice and serve immediately.

## Nutrition Facts per Serving

Calories 172 | Fats 13.57g | Carbs 6.65g | Net Carbs 3.65g | Protein 5.76g

# Chaffles with Keto Ice Cream

Prep time: 10 minutes | Cook time: 14 minutes | Serves: 2

## Ingredients:

- 1 egg, beaten
- ½ cup finely grated mozzarella cheese
- ¼ cup almond flour
- 2 tbsp swerve confectioner's sugar
- 1/8 tsp xanthan gum
- Low-carb ice cream (flavor of your choice) for serving

## Instructions:

1. Preheat the waffle iron.
2. In a medium bowl, mix all the ingredients except the ice cream.
3. Open the iron and add half of the mixture. Close and cook until crispy, 7 minutes.
4. Transfer the chaffle to a plate and make second one with the remaining batter.
5. On each chaffle, add a scoop of low carb ice cream, fold into half-moons and enjoy.

## Nutrition Facts per Serving

Calories 89 | Fats 6.48g | Carbs 1.67g | Net Carbs 1.37g | Protein 5.91g

# Strawberry Shortcake Chaffle Bowls

Prep time: 10 minutes | Cook time: 28 minutes | Serves: 4

## Ingredients:

- 1 egg, beaten
- ½ cup finely grated mozzarella cheese
- 1 tbsp almond flour
- ¼ tsp baking powder
- 2 drops cake batter extract
- 1 cup cream cheese, softened
- 1 cup fresh strawberries, sliced
- 1 tbsp sugar-free maple syrup

## Instructions:

1. Preheat a waffle bowl maker and grease lightly with cooking spray.
2. Meanwhile, in a medium bowl, whisk all the ingredients except the cream cheese and strawberries.
3. Open the iron, pour in half of the mixture, cover, and cook until crispy, 6 to 7 minutes.
4. Remove the chaffle bowl onto a plate and set aside.
5. Make a second chaffle bowl with the remaining batter.
6. To serve, divide the cream cheese into the chaffle bowls and top with the strawberries.
7. Drizzle the filling with the maple syrup and serve.

## Nutrition Facts per Serving

Calories 235 | Fats 20.62g | Carbs 5.9g | Net Carbs 5g | Protein 7.51g

# Chaffles with Raspberry Syrup

Prep time: 10 minutes | Cook time: 38 minutes | Serves: 4

## Ingredients:

### For the chaffles:

- 1 egg, beaten
- ½ cup finely shredded cheddar cheese
- 1 tsp almond flour
- 1 tsp sour cream

### For the raspberry syrup:

- 1 cup fresh raspberries
- ¼ cup swerve sugar
- ¼ cup water
- 1 tsp vanilla extract

## Instructions:

### For the chaffles:

1. Preheat the waffle iron.
2. Meanwhile, in a medium bowl, mix the egg, cheddar cheese, almond flour, and sour cream.
3. Open the iron, pour in half of the mixture, cover, and cook until crispy, 7 minutes.
4. Remove the chaffle onto a plate and make another with the remaining batter.

### For the raspberry syrup:

5. Meanwhile, add the raspberries, swerve sugar, water, and vanilla extract to a medium pot. Set over low heat and cook until the raspberries soften and sugar becomes syrupy. Occasionally stir while mashing the raspberries as you go. Turn the heat off when your desired consistency is achieved and set aside to cool.
6. Drizzle some syrup on the chaffles and enjoy when ready.

## Nutrition Facts per Serving

Calories 105 | Fats 7.11g | Carbs 4.31g | Net Carbs 2.21g | Protein 5.83g

# Chaffle Cannoli

Prep time: 15 minutes | Cook time: 28 minutes | Serves: 4

## Ingredients:

### For the chaffles:

- 1 large egg
- 1 egg yolk
- 3 tbsp butter, melted
- 1 tbsp swerve confectioner's
- 1 cup finely grated Parmesan cheese
- 2 tbsp finely grated mozzarella cheese

### For the cannoli filling:

- ½ cup ricotta cheese
- 2 tbsp swerve confectioner's sugar
- 1 tsp vanilla extract
- 2 tbsp unsweetened chocolate chips for garnishing

## Instructions:

1. Preheat the waffle iron.
2. Meanwhile, in a medium bowl, mix all the ingredients for the chaffles.
3. Open the iron, pour in a quarter of the mixture, cover, and cook until crispy, 7 minutes.
4. Remove the chaffle onto a plate and make 3 more with the remaining batter.

### Meanwhile, for the cannoli filling:

5. Beat the ricotta cheese and swerve confectioner's sugar until smooth. Mix in the vanilla.
6. On each chaffle, spread some of the filling and wrap over.
7. Garnish the creamy ends with some chocolate chips.
8. Serve immediately.

## Nutrition Facts per Serving

Calories 308 | Fats 25.05g | Carbs 5.17g | Net Carbs 5.17g | Protein 15.18g

# Blueberry Chaffles

Prep time: 10 minutes | Cook time: 28 minutes | Serves: 4

## Ingredients:

- 1 egg, beaten
- ½ cup finely grated mozzarella cheese
- 1 tbsp cream cheese, softened
- 1 tbsp sugar-free maple syrup + extra for topping
- ½ cup blueberries
- ¼ tsp vanilla extract

## Instructions:

1. Preheat the waffle iron.
2. In a medium bowl, mix all the ingredients.
3. Open the iron, lightly grease with cooking spray and pour in a quarter of the mixture.
4. Close the iron and cook until golden brown and crispy, 7 minutes.
5. Remove the chaffle onto a plate and set aside.
6. Make the remaining chaffles with the remaining mixture.
7. Drizzle the chaffles with maple syrup and serve afterward.

## Nutrition Facts per Serving

Calories 137 | Fats 9.07g | Carbs 4.02g | Net Carbs 3.42g | Protein 9.59g

# Nutter Butter Chaffles

Prep time: 15 minutes | Cook time: 14 minutes | Serves: 2

## Ingredients:

### For the chaffles:

- 2 tbsp sugar-free peanut butter powder
- 2 tbsp maple (sugar-free) syrup
- 1 egg, beaten
- ¼ cup finely grated mozzarella cheese
- ¼ tsp baking powder
- ¼ tsp almond butter
- ¼ tsp peanut butter extract
- 1 tbsp softened cream cheese

### For the frosting:

- ½ cup almond flour
- 1 cup peanut butter
- 3 tbsp almond milk
- ½ tsp vanilla extract
- ½ cup maple (sugar-free) syrup

## Instructions:

1. Preheat the waffle iron.
2. Meanwhile, in a medium bowl, mix all the ingredients until smooth.
3. Open the iron and pour in half of the mixture.
4. Close the iron and cook until crispy, 6 to 7 minutes.
5. Remove the chaffle onto a plate and set aside.
6. Make a second chaffle with the remaining batter.
7. While the chaffles cool, make the frosting.
8. Pour the almond flour in a medium saucepan and stir-fry over medium heat until golden.
9. Transfer the almond flour to a blender and top with the remaining frosting ingredients. Process until smooth.
10. Spread the frosting on the chaffles and serve afterward.

## Nutrition Facts per Serving

Calories 239 | Fats 15.48g | Carbs 17.42g | Net Carbs 15.92g | Protein 7.52g

# Chaffled Brownie Sundae

Prep time: 12 minutes | Cook time: 30 minutes | Serves: 4

## Ingredients:

### For the chaffles:

- 2 eggs, beaten
- 1 tbsp unsweetened cocoa powder
- 1 tbsp erythritol
- 1 cup finely grated mozzarella cheese

### For the topping:

- 3 tbsp unsweetened chocolate, chopped
- 3 tbsp unsalted butter
- ½ cup swerve sugar
- Low-carb ice cream for topping
- 1 cup whipped cream for topping
- 3 tbsp sugar-free caramel sauce

## Instructions:

### For the chaffles:

1. Preheat the waffle iron.
2. Meanwhile, in a medium bowl, mix all the ingredients for the chaffles.
3. Open the iron, pour in a quarter of the mixture, cover, and cook until crispy, 7 minutes.
4. Remove the chaffle onto a plate and make 3 more with the remaining batter.
5. Plate and set aside.

### For the topping:

6. Meanwhile, melt the chocolate and butter in a medium saucepan with occasional stirring, 2 minutes.

### To serve:

7. Divide the chaffles into wedges and top with the ice cream, whipped cream, and swirl the chocolate sauce and caramel sauce on top.
8. Serve immediately.

## Nutrition Facts per Serving

Calories 165 | Fats 11.39g | Carbs 3.81g | Net Carbs 2.91g | Protein 12.79g

# Brie and Blackberry Chaffles

Prep time: 15 minutes | Cook time: 36 minutes | Serves: 4

## Ingredients:

### *For the chaffles:*

- 2 eggs, beaten
- 1 cup finely grated mozzarella cheese

### *For the topping:*

- 1 ½ cups blackberries
- 1 lemon, 1 tsp zest and 2 tbsp juice
- 1 tbsp erythritol
- 4 slices Brie cheese

## Instructions:

### *For the chaffles:*

1. Preheat the waffle iron.
2. Meanwhile, in a medium bowl, mix the eggs and mozzarella cheese.
3. Open the iron, pour in a quarter of the mixture, cover, and cook until crispy, 7 minutes.
4. Remove the chaffle onto a plate and make 3 more with the remaining batter.
5. Plate and set aside.

### *For the topping:*

6. Preheat the oven to 350 F and line a baking sheet with parchment paper.
7. In a medium pot, add the blackberries, lemon zest, lemon juice, and erythritol. Cook until the blackberries break and the sauce thickens, 5 minutes. Turn the heat off.
8. Arrange the chaffles on the baking sheet and place two Brie cheese slices on each. Top with blackberry mixture and transfer the baking sheet to the oven.
9. Bake 2 to 3 minutes until the cheese melts.
10. Remove from the oven, allow cooling and serve afterward.

## Nutrition Facts per Serving

Calories 576 | Fats 42.22g | Carbs 7.07g | Net Carbs 3.67g | Protein 42.35g

Made in the USA
Monee, IL
26 February 2023

28768800R00061